Legends and Stories

FROM THE APPALACHIAN TRAIL

STEVE STOCKTON
JASON KENT

FREE REIGN

ISBN 13: 979-8-89234-008-3

Free Reign Publishing, LLC
San Diego, CA

Contents

Introduction   v

Chapter 1   1
DUDLEYTOWN: THE CURSED VILLAGE

Chapter 2   7
CIVIL WAR GHOSTS

Chapter 3   13
THE FLATWOODS MONSTER

Chapter 4   17
THE GIGGLING GHOSTS OF SINKING CREEK

Chapter 5   21
BELL WITCH

Chapter 6   25
THE MOON-EYED PEOPLE OF APPALACHIA

Chapter 7   31
THE HAUNTED BLUE GHOST TUNNEL

Chapter 8   35
*THE TRAGIC STORY OF THE PIERCE POND
GHOST*

Chapter 9   39
THE ROANOKE COLONY GHOSTS

Publisher's Excerpt   43

Publisher's Excerpt 2   57

Chapter 10   63
THE PINK LADY OF CARTER COUNTY

Chapter 11   67
*WHISPERING SPIRITS OF THE GREAT
SMOKY MOUNTAINS*

Chapter 12   71
TALE OF THE TAILYPO

Chapter 13   75
HOOTIN' ANNIE

Chapter 14   79
LUCY OF ROARING FORK

Chapter 15   83
MOTHMAN

Chapter 16   87
BIGFOOT

Chapter 17   99
SERIAL KILLERS ON THE TRAIL

Chapter 18   109
MISSING PEOPLE CASES

Conclusion   121
About the Author   125
Also by Steve Stockton   127
Also by Free Reign Publishing   131

Introduction

The Appalachian Trail, often referred to as simply the AT, is one of the longest hiking trails in the world at approximately 2,200 miles. It passes through 14 states along the crest of the Appalachian Mountains, from Springer Mountain in Georgia to Mount Katahdin in Maine. The trail attracts between two to three million hikers every year who come to experience its stunningly diverse landscapes and pristine wilderness.

The AT offers a variety of ecosystems and microclimates as it winds through national forests, parks, quaint towns, as well as lakes, rivers and waterfalls. The changing elevation and latitude means the climate ranges from warm and humid down south to cool and Alpine-like up north. The biodiversity along the trail is immense, with over

2,200 documented rare, threatened and endangered species.

Considered a perfect hiking destination for all levels, sections of the AT are accessible via day hikes while through hikers attempt to complete the entire end-to-end journey. But despite its beauty and popularity, some remote and isolated sections of the trail have a dark side. The secluded nature has provided opportunity for disturbing crimes over the years. Since the first recorded murder in 1974, there have been around a dozen homicides, as well as numerous assaults, on or near the AT.

It is in these desolate mountains and thick forests where hikers have had chilling experiences that give rise to scary stories and urban legends. This book explores the history, myths and folklore surrounding the Appalachian Trail, from haunted huts to mysterious creatures said to stalk the woods. It delves into true tales of disaster, tragedy and the unexplained that have occurred along this legendary footpath. Learn about the notorious murders and crimes, disappearances and odd occurrences that form the basis for frightening AT legends passed between generations of hikers.

The Appalachian Trail holds a rich history and ethereal beauty, but also secrets, mysteries and horrors waiting to be uncovered. This book peels back the layers to present

the strange and lurid stories from the legendary
Appalachian Trail.

- Steve Stockton

One

DUDLEYTOWN: THE CURSED VILLAGE

THE QUIET TOWN OF CORNWALL, Connecticut was settled in the mid-18th century much like many other parts of the state during that era. The first Dudleys, arriving from England via Guilford, came to the Litchfield Hills region of northwestern Connecticut in 1747. They played a pivotal role in forming a prosperous community then known as Alsbury.

The Dudley family originally lived in and around Guilford. Three Dudley brothers - William, Thomas and David - made the decision to move their families to the wilderness frontier stretching from the small settlement of Salisbury into the northwest hills. Leaders of the expedition, the Dudley brothers had received grants for land in the area and also hoped to profit from the iron ore recently discovered in the region.

In the summer of 1747, the Dudleys along with fifteen other families from Guilford journeyed to the remote hills and founded the town that would become known as Alsbury. They were drawn by the prospects of abundant natural resources, especially iron ore critical to the production of tools, machinery, and other implements. The Dudleys established an iron works, forge and sawmill along the East Aspetuck River to harness water power for these industries.

The settlement grew as more colonists arrived, clearing the wooded land to build homesteads and farms. By 1753, the prosperous community had its own meeting house centered around a village green, with the Dudleys constructing the first house on the western side. The local iron works, led by the Dudleys, was furnishing iron products to towns throughout Connecticut and beyond. Alsbury and its industries continued expanding into the 1760s and 70s.

But as the decades passed, Alsbury's fortunes gradually declined due to a confluence of factors. The seemingly limitless woodlands were being depleted, reducing available lumber and fuel to keep the furnaces burning. Competition from larger iron works opening elsewhere impinged on the town's local industry. And the lure of cheaper, more fertile land in frontier territories like Ohio led to an exodus of younger residents from the stony hills of Connecticut.

The Dudley family in particular was wracked by tragedy and loss during this period. William Dudley's wife and several children died, leaving him embittered. His brother Thomas lost his mind in his old age. And David Dudley's eight children all perished from disease or accidents. By the early 1800s, the Dudleys had all left Alsbury which was shedding population rapidly.

With the death of its leading citizens and collapse of industry, the town slowly withered over the coming decades. The last permanent resident left Alsbury around 1910, leaving it fully abandoned by the start of the 20th century. The empty foundations gradually became enveloped by the surrounding forest which reclaimed the land. All that remained were crumbling chimneys, overgrown wells and root-filled cellars strewn amidst the woods.

By the mid 1900s, the ghost town had gained a reputation as cursed, haunted and associated with misfortune. Some believed the Dudley family had been cursed which led to the demise of the town. There were stories of strange events, apparitions, and a foreboding atmosphere surrounding the former settlement.

Paranormal investigators Ed and Lorraine Warren purportedly filmed a Halloween television special in

Dudleytown during the 1970s in which they dramatically declared the area demonically possessed. This proclamation spawned even more tales of the paranormal, Satanic rituals and ominous energies pervading Dudleytown.

Thrillseekers, amateur ghost hunters and occultists have been drawn to the site along with vandals and those enamored with its dark mystique. Visitors have reported apparitions of ghostly figures, floating lights, unexplained sounds, and an overriding sense of dread. However, descendants of the Dudleys such as Reverend Gary Dudley have disputed the idea of an ancestral curse dooming the town. And historians have found no credible evidence of dark events, violence or tragic occurrences taking place in Dudleytown's past.

Skeptics believe the town's dramatic decline due to economic and demographic factors has fueled imaginative myths of hauntings and curses. But the aura of foreboding still hangs over the long abandoned settlement, now located on private land strictly off limits to visitors. The decaying foundations lie within the Dark Entry Forest owned by an association that aggressively prosecutes trespassers and vandals.

Yet, the legends, rumors and ghostly tales refuse to be laid to rest. People remain fascinated by Dudleytown's tragic fate and the supernatural forces rumored to lurk within its shadows. The ruins seem to exert an irresistible pull on thrillseekers and paranormal enthusiasts deter-mined to unlock its secrets, either through historical inves-tigation or, reportedly, communication with resident spirits.

So the curious, the reckless, and the obsessed continue to find their way to Dudleytown's overgrown cellar holes and decrepit chimneys, primed by its aura of doom. They seek glimpses of resident ghosts, manifestations of evil, or insights into the mystery of how a once-thriving commu-nity met such a sad and ominous end. While definitive evidence proves elusive, the magnetic aura of Dudleytown prevails, keeping alive its legends and air of foreboding. The wooded realm of ghosts and shadowy evil refuses to release its hold on visitors' imaginations.

Two

CIVIL WAR GHOSTS

THE APPALACHIAN NATIONAL SCENIC TRAIL, often called simply the Appalachian Trail or the AT, stretches over 2,190 miles from Springer Mountain in Georgia to Mount Katahdin in Maine. As the longest hiking-only trail in the world, it passes through some of the most remote and wild terrain in the eastern United States. But many hikers discover that they are not always alone on the trail. In certain sections that pass through areas of Civil War battles, the ghosts of soldiers still walk the paths and haunt the forests and fields.

One area known for its Civil War ghosts is the 40-mile section in Maryland that stretches from Pen Mar Park south to Gathland State Park at Crampton's Gap. Three bloody battles were fought here in September 1862 as Confederate General Robert E. Lee's first invasion of the north. The Battle of South Mountain took place on September 14th as Union forces attempted to push the Confederates back. The Battle of Antietam, the bloodiest single-day battle in American history with over 22,000 casualties, occurred on September 17th. And the Battle of Shepherdstown happened on September 19th as Lee's army retreated back across the Potomac.

With so much death and violence concentrated in this region over just a few days, many believe it has left an imprint on the land that haunts it to this day. Hikers through Maryland report hearing ghostly gunfire echoing off the mountains, smelling the smoke from long-extinguished cannon fire, and even seeing tent cities with Confederate soldiers that disappear when approached. The famous Burnside Bridge over Antietam Creek is said to replay the battle, with soldiers in blue and gray uniforms firing at each other before fading away into the night.

One of the most haunted spots is the Farm of Daniel Wise. It is located near Fox's Gap, the site of fierce fighting on September 14th. The story goes that Wise, a supporter of the Union, was so embittered by the Confederate invaders that he rounded up the bodies of dead Rebel soldiers after the battle and threw them into his well. It is said that as many as 58 bodies were disposed down the well, rotting away and poisoning the water. Since that time, many have reported seeing ghostly figures in tattered gray uniforms wandering around the Wise farm and standing over the well, condemned to haunt the place of their desecrated burial for eternity. Screams and moans are also said to emit from the well late at night.

Wise Farm is private property now, but a hiking trail passes close by. Hikers have reported uneasy feelings and the sense they are being watched as they walk the trail near the property. Unexplained cold spots, misty figures darting behind trees, and odd sounds have occurred here. A ghostly campfire sometimes appears off in the woods, with haggard transparent soldiers sitting around it before blinking out. The figures are thought to be the discarded Confederate dead from Wise's well trying in vain to warm their eternal coldness.

A similarly creepy location is the grounds of the Burnside Bridge Civil War Museum about 1 mile north of the famous bridge itself. The museum is housed in what was once the Antietam Iron Works, which served as a field hospital during and after the Battle of Antietam. Beams still show scores carved into them by convalescing Union soldiers. The Iron Works saw hundreds of amputations and many deaths from wounds and disease.

Staff and visitors at the museum report all kinds of unusual phenomena. Disembodied screams are often heard echoing outside at night, along with pleas for help or cries for water. Spectral figures in both Union blue and

Confederate gray have been seen wandering the grounds. Phantom campfires like the one seen at Wise Farm also appear from time to time. Strange mists or fogs form out of nowhere and move against the wind. And camera batteries are inexplicably drained despite having been fully charged.

Rangers at the Antietam National Battlefield nearby also report uncanny events related to the bloody fighting here. They have seen ghost soldiers moving silently through the woods just out of clear sight. The smell of gunpowder is often noticed by visitors when no reenactments are taking place. And certain sensitive individuals say they feel overwhelmingly sorrowful when standing by the mass graves of unknown soldiers in the cemetery.

Other areas of paranormal activity include Crampton's Gap, where Confederate soldiers killed by a deadly artillery barrage are said to still inhabit the slope. Across Pleasant Valley at Elk Ridge, Union cavalrymen are reported to endlessly charge up the western slope towards an enemy that is no longer there. And the streets of Sharpsburg, which became overwhelmed with dead and dying men after Antietam, are still thought to replay the mournful cries of the wounded at night.

Explanations for these ghosts vary. Some say it is a kind of recording imprinted in the environment from such intense events. Skeptics say it is just people's overactive imaginations in creepy, historic places. But those who believe say that the scale of violence and death during those September days in 1862 was so immense that many souls were not ready or willing to move on.

Brian Begeman, a local historian who offers ghost tours of the Antietam battlefield each October, explained it this way: "When men by the tens of thousands are ripped from this mortal coil in such a short period, they leave behind echoes. It makes an imprint, like a voice recorded on a record. Replay the record, and you can still hear those voices. Every autumn when the leaves fall and the season turns, it's like replaying that record here. And the lost come out once more to wander back to their battle, still looking for rest."

So if you find yourself hiking along this storied section of the Appalachian Trail, keep your eyes and ears open as the sun goes down or mist gathers. You might just have your own ghostly encounter with the spirits of America's bloodiest war who are still haunting the land where they gave their last full measure. Some are simply lost, while others seem to want to tell their stories to any who will listen. But engage them respectfully if you dare, for the dead of Antietam and South Mountain lived and died in a fearsome time that must not be forgotten. Their ghosts serve as reminders of this history, etched into the memory of these wild and haunted places.

Three

THE FLATWOODS MONSTER

THE SMALL TOWN of Flatwoods sits tucked away in the hills of West Virginia's Braxton County. Life there was simple but idyllic for the farming families that called Flatwoods home in the early 1950s. But one autumn night in 1952, terror descended from the stars above and stirred the town to frenzy. The legend of the Flatwoods Monster was born – an enduring mystery that still haunts this remote place.

The evening of September 12th began like any other in Flatwoods. As darkness fell, some local boys were playing football at the town school. Among them were Eddie and Fred May, Tommy Hyer, and national guardsman Eugene Lemon. When a bright light streaked across the night sky around 7:15pm, they paused their game to watch. It arched overhead before appearing to come down on a hilltop belonging to farmer G. Bailey Fischer.

Determined to investigate, the boys headed to the home of Kathleen May, Eddie and Fred's mother. The excited boys convinced Kathleen, her friend Odyle Nicholson, and two of Odyle's teenaged sons – Ronnie Shaver and Neil Nunley – to join them in a search for where the object fell on Fischer's property. Armed with flashlights, the group of now eleven hiked into the darkened hills.

As they climbed the wooded ridge, they could see a pulsating red light glowing ahead and drifted towards it. But halfway up the hillside, the group halted in their tracks at a horrific sight. Looming above them was a massive creature unlike anything they had seen before.

Kathleen May later described it as being at least 10 feet tall with a red, round face shaped like the Ace of Spades. It had bulging green eyes that glowed faintly, as well as clothing that resembled a dark pleated skirt. Odyle Nicholson claimed it appeared to have no visible arms or mouth. Some witnesses reported a shrill hissing noise and a pungent mist that burned their eyes and noses.

Overcome with terror, the group fled down the hillside, stumbling over rocks and logs in their panicked retreat. The younger boys were screeching and sobbing hysterically. When they reached town, they rushed into the local tavern and breathlessly told their incredible tale. The sheriff's office was soon called, launching an investigation that would stir national intrigue.

Police searched the hilltop that night but found no monster. What they did discover was a thick, putrid odor in the area where the creature had been spotted. They also located a section of flattened grass and vegetation, indicating something large had passed through. By morning, rampant speculation was swirling through Flatwoods about what exactly had terrified the witnesses.

News of the incident spread rapidly, eventually reaching UFO researchers and paranormal investigators. Explanations ranged from an extraterrestrial visitor to some unknown cryptid or mutated monster. Some centered on a meteor crash, suggesting mutated wildlife or radiation effects. As witnesses were interviewed on national radio shows, Flatwoods became obsessed with solving the mystery.

Local police first suspected a meteor or downed aircraft, but searches turned up empty. When the Air Force looked into aviation incidents, they found no crashes in the area that night. UFO enthusiasts arrived, scouring the hills for alien evidence but finding none. The furor eventually died down in Flatwoods, but the legend of the monster endured over generations.

The creature's origins remain contested today. Skeptics argue it was a barn owl perched on a branch that the group misidentified, with hysteria fueling their monster sighting. But other details match no known earthly animal, keeping the possibility of the alien explanation alive. Over 70 years later, the true nature of the beast spotted on the Fischer farm hills remains an enigma.

The night of mystery and terror left a permanent mark on Flatwoods and its residents. While the Flatwoods Monster has become a quirky claim to fame for the town, an air of unease still lingers on the hilltop where the horrified witnesses encountered that haunting red-faced specter. For many, the memory and mystery of that September night remains as vivid and frightening as the day it happened.

The legend endures as one of the most compelling early UFO cases. While its validity is still contested, it helped cement the era's obsession with flying saucers, aliens and the paranormal. For students of paranormal Americana, the Flatwoods Monster is an essential chapter in the evolving chronicle of unexplained encounters and creatures perhaps not of this earth. Its mystique lives on for both serious investigators and lovers of classic Fortean tales.

Four

THE GIGGLING GHOSTS OF SINKING CREEK

ALONG A REMOTE SECTION of Virginia's Appalachian Trail near Sinking Creek, an unsettling sound sometimes echoes through the woods - the playful laughter of unseen children. According to local legend, these disembodied giggles and voices belong to the ghosts of three young siblings who perished in the forest over a century ago.

The story stems from a homesteading family named the Wanes who moved to the Sinking Creek area in the early 1900s to setup a small farm. Eugene and Emma Wane brought their three young children - two boys named Edwin and Paul aged 8 and 6, and 4 year-old daughter Mary. The Wanes built a humble cabin and did their best to carve out a living by growing crops and raising livestock.

As the children got older, they were allowed to explore the surrounding woods while their parents tended the farm. The forest with its babbling creeks and rocky outcroppings became the kids' playground. But in the summer of 1909, tragedy struck the Wane family.

After lunch one sunny July day, Edwin, Paul, and Mary asked if they could go play by Sinking Creek. Despite knowing the dangers that lurked in the untamed wilderness, Emma reluctantly agreed. She watched her giggling children skip into the trees on the path leading to the creek. But that evening, the Wane children failed to return home.

Emma and Eugene grew anxious as dusk fell and they had still not appeared. The couple searched frantically through the night and into the next day aided by concerned neighbors. But not a trace of the missing children could be found, save for Mary's doll discovered by the creek's edge.

Weeks passed with no further sign of Edwin, Paul, and Mary Wane. Most gave up hope that they could have survived long alone in the woods. Bears and other wild animals were known to roam the backcountry, and many assumed a tragic animal attack was inevitable. The Wanes were forced to accept they had likely lost all their children.

But over the years, hikers have reported hearing the voices of children near Sinking Creek - laughing, singing, and calling each other's names. The sounds always eventually fade away into silence. Some swearing they've seen ghostly visages of two young boys and girl playing in a small meadow before disappearing. These unsettling encounters are believed to be the spirits of the lost Wane children.

Skeptics say the giggles and sightings are just imagination combined with natural sounds of the forest. But paranormal investigators and psychic mediums who have visited the area say a deep sense of sadness and regret lingers over the unknown fate of the children. And that the Wanes' ghosts remain eternally youthful and playful, unaware of their tragic end.

Believers say the Wane children met their demise in these woods, but their spirits cling to their old play place, maintaining the innocence of childhood by laughing and playing. Others posit their ghosts seek to lure in the living, hoping someone might finally find them and lead them home after being lost for so long.

Whatever the origins of the giggling ghosts, their presence continues to unsettle visitors along Sinking Creek. So next time you are hiking this lonely stretch of trail, keep alert for sounds of play in the woods. Stop and listen closely and you may just hear the Wane children giggling as if still lost in an endless game only they can see and understand.

Five

BELL WITCH

IN THE EARLY 19TH CENTURY, nestled within the rural landscape of Adams, Tennessee, a peculiar and unsettling tale unfolded. It was a tale of inexplicable events, spectral voices, and a malevolent presence that would come to be known as the Bell Witch. This chapter delves into the well-documented account of the Bell Witch haunting, drawing from historical records and eyewitness testimonies.

Origins of the Haunting:

The story of the Bell Witch centers around the Bell family, headed by John Bell and his wife Lucy. The family, including their children, settled in the Red River community in Robertson County, Tennessee, in the early 1800s.

Life seemed ordinary for the Bells until around 1817 when strange occurrences began to disrupt their peaceful existence.

The first signs of the Bell Witch's presence manifested as unexplained noises. Knocking and scratching sounds would echo through the Bell home, seemingly originating from within the walls. At first, the family dismissed these disturbances as mere quirks of their rustic homestead. However, as time passed, the phenomena escalated.

Objects in the house began to move seemingly of their own accord. Furniture would slide across the floor, bedsheets would be ripped away from sleeping occupants, and invisible hands would slap, pinch, and scratch family members. These inexplicable occurrences left the Bell family bewildered and frightened.

The Voice of the Bell Witch

One of the most chilling aspects of the Bell Witch haunting was the entity's ability to speak. The entity often addressed itself as "Kate," claiming to be the spirit of Kate Batts, a deceased neighbor of the Bells. Kate Batts had reportedly harbored a grudge against John Bell, alleging that he had cheated her in a land purchase deal.

Kate's voice was described as a combination of a shrill woman's voice and a harsh, guttural tone. It could engage in conversations, recite Bible verses, and even sing hymns. This spectral voice displayed a deep knowledge of the family's personal affairs and secrets, leaving no doubt that it was more than a simple prank or natural occurrence.

As time passed, the Bell Witch's malevolence became increasingly evident. It particularly targeted John Bell and his daughter, Betsy. The entity tormented them both physically and psychologically, often making cruel and taunting remarks. Betsy, in particular, bore the brunt of the entity's aggression, with her hair being pulled and her face slapped by invisible hands.

One of the most tragic and mysterious events associated with the Bell Witch legend is the death of John Bell. In 1820, John Bell fell gravely ill under circumstances that left the family and the community puzzled. He suffered from paralysis and showed symptoms that defied medical explanation. Throughout his illness, the Bell Witch claimed responsibility for his suffering and eventual demise.

John Bell passed away on December 20, 1820, and it is said that the Bell Witch rejoiced at his death, singing a song of victory. The entity proclaimed that it would return in seven years, a prophecy that left the Bell family deeply unsettled.

· · ·

The End of the Haunting

True to the Bell Witch's word, the disturbances gradually subsided after John Bell's death. The entity seemed to lose interest in tormenting the family and eventually departed. The Bell family and their community were left with a haunting legacy that would continue to fascinate and perplex generations to come.

The Bell Witch legend endures as a captivating piece of American folklore, sparking debates among skeptics and believers alike. The accounts and testimonies surrounding the Bell Witch haunting have been meticulously documented over the years, ensuring that the story remains a significant and enigmatic chapter in the annals of the supernatural.

THE MOON-EYED PEOPLE OF APPALACHIA

Both Appalachian folk tales and Cherokee legends suggest that there could be a group of pale-skinned humanoids known as the moon-eyed people hiding in the Appalachian range. The moon-eyed people are commonly linked to the small town of Murphy, North Carolina. According to legend, they have a short, stout build and white skin, bearded faces, and large blue eyes. Their eyes were said to be susceptible to the sun, making them nocturnal creatures and earning them the moniker "moon-eyed."

According to legend, the indigenous Native American tribes would wait for the full moon to drive out the moon-eyed people from their underground caves. The bright light would weaken them, forcing them to flee to other areas of Appalachia. The moon-eyed people, unlike other

Appalachian monsters, were believed to be a unique and distinct race of people rather than supernatural entities. It's believed that the moon-eyed people were actually European settlers. However, the legends surrounding them originate from a time well before Christopher Columbus' arrival in America.

Some theories suggest the moon-eyed people were descendants of Prince Madoc, a Welsh prince who allegedly sailed to America in 1170, over 300 years before Columbus. Others believe they were a wayward Viking clan that traveled to the Americas. Another theory is that they were an albino offshoot of the Cherokee tribe.

The first written account of the moon-eyed people comes from Cherokee scholar James Mooney in the 19th century. Mooney recorded several tales passed down through oral tradition describing the moon-eyed people as having light-colored skin, blond hair, and large eyes. According to Mooney, the Cherokee tribes drove the moon-eyed people from their native lands after long wars. The surviving moon-eyed people were forced to retreat into the remote mountains of Tennessee, North Carolina, and Georgia.

In Cherokee legends, the moon-eyed people are said to have lived in massive cave cities carved from underground mountains. These cave dwellings were only accessible through hidden entrances. The moon-eyed people reportedly came out at night to raid Cherokee settlements for food and provisions. To avoid being seen, they always attacked under the cover of darkness or fog. That is why the Cherokee would light torches and stay awake when fog appeared, to keep watch for attacks.

Some accounts claim the moon-eyed people were adept at magicas and could make themselves invisible. Other stories describe them as small, child-sized people who wore gray clothing and spoke a language unknown to the Cherokee. Their names for each other sounded like bird calls.

According to legend, the Cherokee tribes grew tired of the moon-eyed people's nighttime raids and launched an attack against their hidden cave cities. However, they could not find the hidden entrances to the caves. Eventually, after many losses, the Cherokee decided to wait for a bright, sunny day before attacking again. The brightness of the daytime sun weakened the moon-eyed people, allowing the Cherokee warriors to drive them from their mountain homes. The surviving moon-eyed people were forced to flee the Cherokee territory.

Presently, exhibits of the moon-eyed people can be found at the Cherokee County Historical Museum in Murphy, North Carolina. There is a three-foot tall sculpture of two conjoined figures thought to represent moon-eyed people from the early 1840s. Port Mountain, a

Georgia state park near Ellijay, Georgia contains the ruins of an 850-foot long stone wall. It is said to have been constructed by this mysterious tribe of people.

The legend still persists in Appalachian culture. Some say the moon-eyed people never left, but retreated deeper into the ancient cave systems of the Appalachian Mountains. Stories abound of modern encounters with strange pale-skinned people emerging from old mine shafts and caverns. Locals speak of hearing eerie chanting and humming coming from underground. Others claim to have found the small, child-sized remains of moon-eyed people in old burrows and tunnels.

Many towns and landmarks in the Appalachians are named after the moon-eyed people, such as Moon-Eye, Georgia and Moonville Tunnel in Tennessee. Moonville Tunnel is an abandoned railroad tunnel supposedly used by the moon-eyed people to transport goods between their underground cities. It is said to be haunted by the ghosts of moon-eyed children who perished in the tunnel.

The legend of the moon-eyed people continues to captivate the imagination of Appalachian folklore. While most consider the legend just an intriguing myth, there are those who believe the moon-eyed people really did exist at one time hidden away in the vast wilderness of the Appalachians. Some even claim they still dwell there deep underground, rarely emerging from their subterranean world.

Whether real or mythical, the tales of the moon-eyed people reveal the mystery and magic that pervades the ancient mountains and forests of Appalachia. In those mist-shrouded hollows and caverns, nearly anything seems possible. Perhaps among those remote ridges and valleys there still exist secrets yet to be discovered, remnants of a forgotten race of moon-eyed people lost to time.

Seven

THE HAUNTED BLUE GHOST TUNNEL

ALONG A REMOTE SECTION of Virginia's Appalachian Trail winds a dark, narrow tunnel that strikes fear into the hearts of hikers who dare to pass through it. Known as the "Blue Ghost Tunnel", this foreboding underpass is said to be inhabited by the ghosts of dead railroad workers who perished tragically when the tunnel collapsed during construction over a century ago.

The Blue Ghost Tunnel is located near Cumberland Gap, where Virginia, Kentucky, and Tennessee all meet along the trail. It was built in the late 1800s as part of a railroad project connecting the southeastern United States. However, planning errors led to the tunnel being poorly reinforced. When construction was almost completed in 1890, a portion of the unstable tunnel collapsed, killing a dozen or more workers and trapping their bodies deep within the rubble.

The railroad was eventually rerouted and the failed project abandoned. The sealed off tunnel remained largely forgotten for decades. It wasn't until the Appalachian Trail was formally developed in the 1930s that hikers rediscovered the ominous abandoned tunnel. Since then, reports of paranormal encounters have made the tunnel one of the trail's most infamous spots.

The ghosts are said to be the spirits of the dead workers buried within the collapsed tunnel. Hikers have reported seeing glowing blue figures floating near the boarded up entrance. Some have heard mysterious tapping sounds coming from deep inside the mountain as if the spirits are still trying to dig themselves out. Disembodied voices, echoing screams, and the sound of old work songs sung in unison are also commonly reported.

Strange mists or blue glowing orbs appear in photos taken by visitors, allegedly showing the ghosts manifesting. Cellphones and other electronics are known to abruptly lose power or signal when nearing the tunnel as if an otherworldly force is interfering. Some visitors claim their flashlights will flicker off and on erratically or turn blue without explanation. Others say they've had the feeling of being touched, poked, or having their clothes tugged at by invisible presences.

Many sightings occur in the dead of night or early morning hours when the spirits are believed to be most active. But even in broad daylight the tunnel emits an unnatural coldness and sense of dread. Some say the frigidness comes from the ghosts using visitors' body heat to strengthen their supernatural powers. Others suggest it is a warning for the living to stay away. A few visitors have reported being overtaken with a sudden sense of danger or a need to flee the area, as if the spirits were manifesting directly in their minds.

Ghost hunters frequently stake out the Blue Ghost Tunnel hoping to photograph the phantoms or record their disembodied voices using electronic detecting equipment. While some visitors leave offerings or makeshift memorials hoping to appease the spirits, locals advise against such actions. They warn that engaging with the ghosts in any way risks stirring up their wrath when it's better not to disturb them at all.

Park rangers candidly advise avoiding hiking through the tunnel. While the ghosts have never been known to harm living visitors directly, few have emerged from passing through the collapsed underpass without seeing or hearing something unexplained. The heavy atmosphere of dread that hangs over the site is enough to deter most from braving the haunting tunnel, especially when hiking alone in the dead of night.

Whether all the eyewitness reports over the years are to be believed or not, the legend of the Blue Ghost Tunnel continues to send shivers up spines. For believers, the ghosts of the dead workers still haunt their collapsed tomb, resenting any who dare to trespass. Skeptics say the folklore is just an exaggeration of natural phenomena in an eerie tunnel shunned after its tragic failure. But either way, the Blue Ghost Tunnel remains an ominous landmark along the Appalachian Trail steeped in ominous tales warning thrill-seekers to venture through at their own risk.

Eight

THE TRAGIC STORY OF THE PIERCE POND GHOST

IN THE DENSE, remote forests of Maine near Mount Katahdin lies a dark body of water known as Pierce Pond. Named after the family that once lived near its misty shores, this pond is home to the legend of a young woman's spirit that haunts the surrounding woods over a century after her tragic death.

Effie Pierce was just 17 years old when she married a local lumberjack named Asa Pierce in 1887. Asa was 30 when he took the dark-haired beauty as his bride. He carried her over the threshold of a cabin he had built with his own hands near the pond that would soon take his name. Their nearest neighbor was ten long miles away, ensuring their isolation.

At first, Effie was enchanted by her husband and the rugged beauty of her new home. But as the long Maine winters settled in, she grew melancholy. The snows came early that year, cutting them off entirely from nearby villages. Effie felt utterly alone as Asa left each day to log in the frozen forests. At night she was tormented by the howling winds rattling the cabin's timbers.

When spring finally came, Effie begged Asa to move them somewhere less remote. The long winter had broken her spirits. But Asa refused, and soon after left for weeks on end to work a logging contract up north. Effie wandered the woods while he was gone, growing ever more lost in her despair. Locals say it was during this time that she lost the will to go on.

So when Asa returned to the cabin late one night, he was horrified to find Effie's lifeless body suspended by a rope from a rafter. In her agony, she had taken her own young life. Asa buried her beneath a willow tree by the pond and fled the cabin, unable to bear his grief. From then on, Effie's lonely spirit haunted the pond and nearby trails.

Over the decades, visitors to Pierce Pond have reported eerie encounters with what they believe to be Effie's ghost. Hikers see a young woman in a faded 1800s dress with long dark hair beckoning to them from between the trees. She never speaks, but her eyes convey an unfathomable sorrow. At other times, she silently follows walkers along the trails before disappearing into the woods. Campers occasionally glimpse her wandering along the misty shore of the pond at dusk.

Other unsettling occurrences around Pierce Pond are also attributed to Effie's tormented spirit. Whispers in the wind, footsteps trailing behind but leaving no tracks, odd cold spots, and noises like distant sobbing have all unnerved visitors. Some have awoken from dreams of a young woman pleading with them not to leave her alone.

According to legend, Effie remains bound to this melancholy place because she took her own life. Having committed this grievous sin, she is said to be forever lost between the worlds of the living and dead. Trapped in anguish, she reaches out to connect with the living, hoping to find understanding and forgiveness.

While no historical evidence proves Effie Pierce really lived and died there, decades of eerie tales have ensured her legend endures. Peering through the mist hovering over Pierce Pond, one can almost see her ghostly figure gazing back, still longing for peace over a century after her tragic end in the remote Maine woods that became her eternal home.

Nine

THE ROANOKE COLONY GHOSTS

ALONG LONELY STRETCHES of the Appalachian Trail in Virginia wanders the restless spirits of early English settlers who vanished mysteriously over 400 years ago. In 1587, a group of over 100 men, women and children landed at Roanoke Island on North Carolina's coast hoping to establish a permanent British colony. But when a relief ship returned three years later, the settlers had disappeared without a trace. Their fate remains one of history's most puzzling unsolved mysteries.

Ever since, tales have circulated of lost Roanoke colonists turning up deep in the Appalachian Mountains, hundreds of miles inland from where they were abandoned. Were these emaciated strangers who staggered out of the forest dressed in tattered Elizabethan clothes some of the missing settlers? Or are they ghosts of the Roanoke colonists eternally doomed to haunt the wilderness where they met their demise?

In the late 17th century, a group of English settlers sailing up the Chesapeake Bay reported encountering over a dozen men, women and children on the shore dressed in an older style clothing and speaking an earlier form of English. The strangers explained they were the last survivors of an ill-fated colony to the south from decades past. Before more could be learned, they mysteriously vanished into the forest never to be seen again.

Similar accounts persisted in the following decades. Frontiersmen exploring the Appalachian foothills told tales of ghostly figures dressed in pioneer era clothes stumbling along mountain paths before disappearing. Sometimes they would cry out pleas for help or warn travelers to turn back. Native American tribes spoke of a cursed people doomed to wander the mountains forever.

Many legends suggest the Roanoke colonists fled north after facing starvation on the coast, becoming lost in the unfamiliar terrain. Hikers have reported apparitions of starving settlers ravenously digging for roots and berries. They appear confused when spotted, explaining they are searching for forests and villages they passed through weeks before that are no longer there.

Other more chilling accounts propose some colonists were captured and killed by hostile native tribes like the legendary Croatan who were rumored to have wiped out the settlement. Along certain trails, cries and screams echo through the night, as if the sounds of the Lost Colony being slaughtered are eternally relived.

Some have seen glowing white figures floating above the trees and peering down at them, believed to be the spirits of colonists murdered in the forests below. Old bloodstains are said to mysteriously appear and vanish on rocks and trees where victims met their end. Hikers also report unseen footsteps crashing through brush and phantom arrows or spears sailing past their heads.

Paranormal researchers believe the ghosts of the Roanoke settlers still haunt the Appalachian Trail, desperately trying to find a way out of the wilderness that became their grave. Campfires and torch lights spotted deep in uninhabited forests are thought to be the colonists' spirits attempting to signal the living. Cross markings carved into trees and small rock mounds arranged to spell "CRO" serve as their cryptic memorials.

The fate of Virginia's first colonists remains one of early American history's deepest mysteries. But along the Appalachian Trail that traverses their vanishings, echoes of the Lost Colony live on. Are they merely legends borne of the mountains vastness playing tricks on hikers' minds? Or do ghosts of Roanoke's doomed pioneers still roam these ancient hills, unable to rest until their tragic story is finally told? For some, every bend holds the potential for a spectral encounter with America's first ghostly history.

IT CAME AT NIGHT

It was the early summer of 1999, and after getting through a nasty divorce, I decided to move to get as far away from my past as possible. I didn't want to go to a city; instead I desired peace and quiet, somewhere in the countryside, away from people, lights, pollution, you name it. I just wanted some alone time to think through the past four years of my life.

I had always liked the mountains and knew there I'd find what I was looking for. I put most of my belongings in storage and set out to the mountains of Idaho to a small town called Stanley. I found a trailer to rent and settled in right away.

I hadn't moved into the trailer for a week before I was awoken by a loud slap on the outside. I shot up and looked around but couldn't see a thing, as it was pitch black. As anyone who's lived in the mountains can attest, when there's no moon, it's incredibly dark outside. Of course, this makes for spectacular stargazing, but seeing anything without the aid of a flashlight...impossible.

I sat there and listened for a repeat sound to make sure I wasn't just dreaming, but it never came. I nestled back into the covers and went back to sleep.

The next morning, I awoke to find my trash can had been dragged from the side of the trailer and down to the woods; garbage was everywhere. I then knew I hadn't dreamt the sound and chalked it up to a bear. I gathered up the garbage and put the trash can back. I placed a large rock on top and even bungee corded the lid down. I went about my day and thought nothing of it.

That night I again was awoken by a loud slap on the side of the trailer. This time I knew I wasn't dreaming and intended to scare the bear away before it got into my trash again. I tossed the covers off me, grabbed a flashlight I had left on the nightstand, and rushed to the front door. I flipped on the outside light and threw the door open. I clicked on the old Maglite and scanned the front yard. I saw the trash can was how I'd left it. I continued to wave the beam of the light around but saw nothing. Thinking as if the bear could understand me, I cried out, "Don't come back, you hear?"

Satisfied that I had scared the bear away, I closed the door and locked it, turned off the light, and went back to bed. As I lay there staring into the darkness, I felt a sense of pride. I had been raised in the suburbs, but now I was fast becoming a mountain girl and had officially chased away my first bear. I closed my eyes and fell back to sleep.

I don't know what time it was, but I was again awoken by a slap. This time it was at the head of my bed on the outside wall. I opened my eyes but didn't sit up. All I could think was the bear was certainly as stubborn as my ex was, and I'd have to be just as determined to get rid of him as I had my former husband. I swung my legs out of bed, grabbed the flashlight, and clicked it on. When the light splashed across the room, I saw something large step away from the window, which was just over my bed.

Startled, I recoiled and turned the light directly on the window, but whatever had been there was now gone. I assumed the bear was now peering into my window like a sick voyeur. Determined that I'd have to really scare it away this time, I marched to the front door, flipped on the outside light, and threw open the door. The cool air wafted in as well as an odor I wasn't familiar with. The best way to describe it is to say it smelled like old musty or moldy clothes. I cast the beam of the flashlight across the yard and instantly caught sight of something racing into the woods, and from the half-a-second glance, it appeared to be on two legs. I kept the beam on the spot I'd last seen it, but it was gone. I first thought it odd that it was on two legs but remembered that bears sometimes walk on their hind legs.

Like earlier, I hollered, "Go away and leave me alone!" I looked at the trash can and saw that it was fine. Hoping that was enough, I closed the door, but instead of turning the light off, I kept it on and went back to bed.

The next morning I woke to find nothing out of sorts and went about my day until later that afternoon I was out clearing some debris from around the trailer when I discovered two large indentions in the ground just beneath my bedroom window. I examined them more closely, and to my astonishment, they appeared to be large footprints. I shook my head, as I couldn't believe what I was seeing. How could those be footprints and massive ones at that? I didn't take a picture, as I didn't have a digital camera at the time, and if I were to go off of memory, I'd say they were at least fifteen inches in length and had to be seven inches wide. I could make out toes and would guess the prints were two plus inches deep. I stepped back, dumbfounded, looked up, and saw that my window was about eight feet off the ground. I clearly recalled seeing something move in front of the window, so that had to mean that whoever was standing outside my bedroom window was eight feet or more tall. A tinge of fear creeped up on me. None of it made sense. I then began to think it was my ex harassing me. That he somehow found where I lived and was now here causing me trouble. My initial fear gave way to fury and anger. I marched inside the trailer, picked up the phone, and called his mobile phone. The second he answered, I'd give him a piece of my mind.

The phone rang a couple of times and went to voice-mail. Filled with anger, I left a scathing message and hung up. I set the phone back in the cradle and exited the trailer, feeling better about myself. I wouldn't tolerate him harassing me like he had during our last year in marriage. There was no way I'd let him take away from the peace and solitude of my new life.

The afternoon gave way to evening. I grilled a nice steak, popped a beer, and relaxed on a chair, looking north towards the Sawtooth mountains. As the sun set behind the mountains, I found myself gripped by a feeling that someone was watching me. I don't know how to describe why I felt that way, but I could feel it. My sixth sense was telling me someone was in the woods near the tree line. Curious if it was my ex, I got up from my chair, beer in hand, and went down to the edge of the woods. I looked around but couldn't make out anything in the dark shadows of the hulking ponderosas and aspens. I called out my ex's name and finished by saying, "If you keep bothering me, I'll call the sheriff. Do you hear me?"

Of course, there wasn't a reply; in fact, there wasn't any sound at all coming from the woods. I tossed the rest of my beer back and threw the empty bottle. I heard it land, waited for a second to see if I could hear any movement at all, then turned around and went back to my chair. I opened my cooler, took out another beer, popped the top, and sat down to enjoy one last drink before I went inside. I could feel the fatigue of the long day laboring around the yard wearing on me, and before I knew it, I was fast asleep.

I woke suddenly, my body chilled. I was surrounded by the dark of night. I looked around, fearful, as I felt a presence in the darkness. I had no idea how long I'd been asleep, nor what time it was, but something wasn't right. I wanted to get up and move, but I felt frozen in fear. My head swiveled around as my eyes desperately tried to make something out, but I couldn't see a thing except for the brilliant stars above. I craned my head in the direction of the trailer, but the light I thought I had left on was out.

Then I heard it. The sound of footfalls coming towards me from the edge of the woods filled my body with terror. I found the courage to get to my feet and, without a concern for what could be in my way, took off at a sprint towards the trailer. I reached the side, felt my way to the door, opened it, and literally leapt inside. I slammed the door behind me and flipped on the light. I peered through a window in the living room, which over-looked the yard, but didn't see anything. I began to wonder if I was now just hallucinating all of it. Had my divorce been so bad that I now had some sort of PTSD? It took me a few minutes to get my composure and calm down.

Feeling at ease, I went to the sink to get a glass of water. I filled a glass, raised it to my lips to drink, but froze when I peered over the glass. There standing in the window, its black eyes staring at me, was something out of a night-mare. I let out a scream, dropped the glass, and ran back towards my bedroom, thinking this was my safe space. I closed the door and sat down on the floor next to the bed, my knees curled up to my chest, with my arms wrapped around them.

I could feel my heart beating heavily. I knew what I'd seen was not my ex, nor was it a person; it was something else, something sinister looking and big. Because like my bedroom window, the kitchen window over the sink was the same height.

I rocked back and forth, thinking about what I should do. I hadn't thought of bringing any sort of weapon with me. Heck, I had nothing to defend myself.

A loud slap came from the outside wall to my left.

I jumped with fear.

Another loud slap came, this time on the opposite side. That thing was moving around the trailer, and here I was inside with nothing to protect myself. Feeling helpless, I began to pray.

Tapping on the window above my bed startled me. I looked up but saw nothing but a shadow; it was there and looking down on me, I could feel it. Filled with terror, I jumped to my feet and raced out of my bedroom. I darted for the phone, pulled it from the cradle, and dialed 911. The second the phone connected, I begged for help.

The operator told me to calm down and said that a deputy would make it out to me as fast as they could. She, however, gave me the disclaimer that it would probably take about thirty minutes. So much for life in the mountains, I thought.

A sound from the front door hit my ears. I looked and saw the knob turning left, then right.

"Go away!" I screamed. "Leave me alone!"

The 911 operator was still connected and told me to go find a safe place to hide and to expect the deputy as soon as they could make it. She also recommended that if I had a weapon, to get it. I put the phone down, grabbed a knife, and picked up the receiver. The operator told me to go hide, which I did. I dropped the phone and ran back to my bedroom. I drew the blinds and hid in the corner next to the dresser, the knife firmly in my hand.

I still don't know how long it took the deputy to get there, but as I waited, the slapping and bangs kept going on and on, only to stop when I saw the headlights of the deputy's car wash over the trailer.

It took every ounce of control I had not to embrace the deputy and sob in his arms.

After a brief conversation, he investigated the property but couldn't find anything.

I told him emphatically that someone had been outside taunting me, and I gave him a detailed description of what I'd seen in the window.

I could tell he was doubtful of my description; to be honest, I was too. While I had heard of Bigfoot before, I never paid it any attention, nor did I believe they existed. But the more I thought about what I had seen, I came to the only conclusion that what was terrorizing me was just that, a Bigfoot.

He stayed for about forty-five minutes but had to leave. Without finding any evidence of someone currently there, he told me to lock up tight and, like the operator, recommended I go buy a gun.

I watched him leave and prayed that whatever was out there would leave me alone. My prayers were answered, as the rest of the evening was quiet.

The next day I went into town and purchased a shotgun. If this thing was going to come back, I'd at least have the means to protect myself.

The evening came without any issues, as did the night, until once more I was awoken by an incredibly loud thud. This was different than the slaps; it was like something had punched the side of the trailer. I jumped from bed, this time grabbing the shotgun, and went to the corner of the room and squatted down. I hadn't bothered to wear pajamas that night because I had a good feeling I'd have a visitor.

The loud bangs gave way to the entire trailer shuddering as if the thing was trying to tip it over.

I was beyond terrified and didn't know what to do. I

went to the phone and, like the evening before, called 911. The operator once more dispatched a deputy.

As I waited, this time in the darkened living room, the shotgun in my white-knuckled grip, I decided I had to prove I wouldn't be pushed around. I mustered all the courage I had, marched over to the door, turned on the light, threw open the door, leveled the shotgun up towards the sky, and screamed, "If you don't leave me alone, I'll shoot you!" I pulled the trigger.

To my right, just beyond the light, I saw the creature race across the yard towards the woods.

Feeling victorious, I decided not to let up. I pumped the action of the shotgun and once more fired into the sky. "Get out of here!"

I could hear the creature crashing through the woods, the sounds of wood cracking, and heaving footfalls.

Once more I pumped the shotgun and let out a blast. Each time I felt my fear ease up. There wasn't any doubt now that the creature was fearful itself and didn't like the sound of a shotgun.

My fear was now replaced with anger, an anger born of this thing thinking it could torment me, that it could disrupt my new life. No, I wasn't going to have any of that.

The same deputy arrived, but this time he found me in a different state of mind. Against his recommendations, I joined him in searching the property. We found tracks, but he dismissed their being from a creature and said they probably were some teenagers causing havoc. I tried to argue with him, but there wasn't any use. We also found a couple of sizable dents in the siding, no doubt from it hitting the side.

When he left, I was still outside, my shotgun still in my grip. I looked towards the woods and, for good measure, fired once more into the woods. I wanted to make sure it knew I meant business.

I went to bed feeling not as vulnerable. I also ended up not having more trouble that night.

The next day, I went into town to find an electrician. I wanted lights installed all around the trailer with motion sensors. I'd cover every inch and then some; however, I was met with frustration, as I couldn't get the lights installed for a few days.

I arrived home in the middle of the afternoon to find my trash cans not just turned over, but the can itself crushed. I knew what had done it and knew then I was probably in store for some trouble that night. I cleaned up the mess, loaded the shotgun, and prepared for what most likely would be a siege.

To my surprise, nothing happened. I thought I heard some noises like walking around, but no hitting the side of the trailer.

Morning came and with it no issues outside. The next

couple of nights were similar.

The electrician came and installed the lights, giving me a sense of peace. I hadn't had any trouble, and I clearly thought my show of defiance must have warned it from coming up to the house.

Later that night I woke to the lights on the north end of the property turning on. I jumped from my bed and peered out the window to see the creature walking briskly back into the woods. I kept watching for what must have been minutes; then the lights to the south end of the property came on. I craned my head but didn't see anything. After a few more minutes, the lights installed to the west kicked on. I raced to another window and looked out only to see nothing. I assumed the creature was literally testing the perimeter. This thought gave me chills, as it proved it wasn't just an animal but had intellect.

The testing of the perimeter went on for about ten minutes before ceasing for the rest of the night.

I got up the next morning, now determined to find out more, and the best place was to contact the landlord. I reached him and detailed what had been happening. He denied any knowledge but did give me the ability to break the lease early without consequence. I did just that.

While I felt empowered with my shotgun and the lights, my anxiety was riding high. I hadn't come all this way to the mountains to live like this. I packed up and left the next day and never looked back.

I've never since had any experience like that and still live in Idaho. I frequent the woods and hike a lot in the Frank Church Wilderness. I've not shared this story before but thought that after all this time and with the acceptance of Bigfoot increasing, it was time to let people know this creature does exist and can be an inconvenience if you're looking for peace and quiet.

ENCOUNTERS IN THE WOODS: VOLUME 1

STRANGE NATIONAL PARK DISAPPEARANCES:
VOLUME 1

WHAT HAPPENED TO ROBERT BISSELL?

On a serene summer morning in 2010, Robert Bissell, a 57-year-old resident of Portland, Oregon, embarked on what was intended to be a brief respite in the Roaring River Wilderness Area near Rock Lakes above Estacada. Known for his love of solitude and backcountry backpacking, Robert often sought the peace of Oregon's remote areas, a place where he could fish alone, lost in nature's embrace.

On July 12th, as Portland's cityscape faded into the rearview mirror of his white 1989 Nissan Sentra, Robert headed southeast, towards a wilderness that promised both isolation and adventure. He was an experienced hiker, one who understood the call of the wild and respected its rules. Before delving into the wilderness, he filed a permit with the Forest Service, penciling in July 16th as his return date. But the wilderness had other plans, and Robert would not be seen again.

Parking his Sentra at Trailhead 700, Robert set off on Trail 512. He pitched his tent, a solitary sentinel in the vast expanse of green, leaving behind his sleeping bag and gear. With only his fishing rod and tackle, he seemed to intend just a short sojourn, perhaps to wrestle trout from the surrounding lakes.

Days drifted by, and silence ensued. Concern crept into the hearts of those who knew him when he failed to return. On July 19th and again on July 24th, his brother, driven by a growing unease, ventured to the campsite. The tent was as Robert had left it, but of Robert, there was no trace. His brother, grasping the gravity of the situation, reported him missing.

The Clackamas County Sheriff Search and Rescue team, a mosaic of determination and hope, launched a colossal search on July 25th. Their mission spanned eight days, encompassing the Roaring River Wilderness, Rock Lakes Basin, and a labyrinth of trails and lakes. This rugged terrain, untamed and often unforgiving, held its secrets close.

Fellow campers recalled crossing paths with Robert at the start of his journey, his intentions penned in a note left behind. They spoke of a man setting up camp, then departing to fish, his rod and tackle companions in his quest for the lakes' trout.

Flyers fluttered in campgrounds, trailheads, and ranger stations, each a silent plea for information. In Estacada, the whispers of Robert's disappearance echoed through the streets.

Sergeant James Rhodes of the Clackamas County Search and Rescue Unit pondered the possibilities – injury, perhaps, in the rugged expanse of the Rock Lakes Basin. Despite the chill of the nights, Rhodes remained optimistic. "It gets chilly at night, but it's not the kind of weather that pushes people into hypothermia," he stated, even as he acknowledged the absence of cell service in the area.

The search was vast and varied – a fleet of volunteers, professionals, aircraft, rescue dogs, horseback patrols, ATVs, and 4x4 units. They scoured the terrain, eyes keen for any sign of Robert. Six-member teams deployed, their calls and whistles piercing the silence, yet met with no response.

But nature does not yield its mysteries easily. The rough terrain took its toll, evidenced by the search horses that threw their shoes. When the search concluded on August 3rd, Robert remained a whisper in the wilderness, his whereabouts as elusive as the shadows beneath the trees.

Items were found, each raising a flicker of hope, only to be extinguished when Robert's brother, Michael, confirmed they were not his. Campers spoke of seeing Robert, of conversations when he first set up camp, but these anecdotes were mere fragments in a larger, unsolved puzzle.

As if swallowed by the forest itself, Robert's clothing and fishing gear remained undiscovered. The case of Robert Bissell, the man who sought solitude in the Roaring River Wilderness, became a tale of disappearance, a narrative woven into the tapestry of Oregon's wilderness mysteries, leaving a lingering question echoing through the trees: What happened to Robert Bissell?

* * *

STRANGE NATIONAL PARK DISAPPEARANCES: VOLUME 1

Ten

THE PINK LADY OF CARTER COUNTY

NESTLED in the ancient hills of Carter County, Tennessee is the sad legend of the Pink Lady, a ghostly woman doomed to eternally search for her lost lover along the lonely roads in the valley. Tales of her sightings have circulated for over a century, making her one of Tennessee's most captivating and tragic spectral figures.

The story begins with a beautiful young woman named Elvira who fell deeply in love with a handsome gentleman named Percy around the year 1880. Though they were soulmates, Percy was tragically struck with tuberculosis. As his health worsened, he sought treatment at a sanatorium high in the mountains near Elk Mills.

Elvira was devoted to her darling Percy. She rented a nearby cabin so she could visit Percy every day at the sanatorium. The couple continued to exchange love letters when they were apart promising their devotion. But one day, Elvira arrived to find Percy had vanished - the sanatorium claimed no knowledge of his whereabouts.

Distraught, Elvira searched desperately for her lost love but found no trace. Some cruelly gossiped Percy had grown tired of her and ran off with another lady. Heartbroken, Elvira withdrew into her cabin, pining away for Percy until she eventually died of sorrow. Now her restless spirit searches eternally for her dear Percy.

Eyewitnesses claim to have seen the ghost of Elvira drifting along the remote mountain roads around Elk Mills, ever-faithful in her search for Percy. She is described as wearing a light pink gown and bonnet, thus earning her the name "The Pink Lady." Some catch glimpses of her crying softly before she fades away. Drivers have stopped to offer her a ride, only for her to disappear once inside the vehicle.

A chilling encounters occur when she is spotted floating in front of cars, forcing drivers to swerve dangerously to avoid hitting her. Some say if you stop and ask about Percy, her face will light up joyfully thinking he has sent you. Skeptics claim she is just a legend, but longtime Carter County residents insist she is real - a sad ghost still longing for her true love.

So if you're driving the old mountain roads around Elk

Mills late at night, keep watch for a figure in pink walking along the roadside. It just may be the devoted spirit of Elvira, the Pink Lady of Carter County, tirelessly continuing her search for her darling Percy over a century after they were tragically torn apart.

Eleven

WHISPERING SPIRITS OF THE GREAT SMOKY MOUNTAINS

THE GREAT SMOKY MOUNTAINS, a subrange of the Appalachian Mountains, are not only known for their mesmerizing beauty but also for the rich history and folklore they embody, particularly tales stemming from the Native Cherokee people. The Cherokee, original inhabitants of these lands, believed that the Smokies were sacred and inhabited by various spirits, each with its distinct characteristics and lore.

The Cherokee held a deep spiritual connection with the Smoky Mountains, considering them a sanctuary of ancient wisdom and supernatural powers. They believed that the mist-covered peaks and dense, mysterious forests were home to spirits that could influence the natural world and the lives of individuals.

Among the spirits believed to inhabit the Smokies are

the Yunwi Tsundi (Little People), the Nunnehi, and other unnamed entities that represent the good and malevolent forces in the world.

Yunwi Tsundi (Little People)

The Yunwi Tsundi, translating to "Little People", are benevolent spirits crucial in Cherokee mythology. Described as small, dwarf-like beings, they are said to live deep within the forests and rocky areas of the mountains. According to lore, these spirits are guardians of the land, protecting the wildlife and helping lost travelers find their way. However, they are also known to be mischievous, sometimes leading people astray or borrowing objects that are seldom returned.

Nunnehi

The Nunnehi, often referred to as the Immortals, are another group of spirits deeply embedded in Cherokee folklore. These supernatural beings are considered the protectors of the Cherokee people, often intervening during times of crisis or war. They reside in the highlands of the Smokies, invisible to the human eye, yet their presence is often felt. Stories tell of their ethereal music and laughter echoing through the mountains, a sign of their eternal celebration of life.

Malevolent Entities

While many spirits are seen as protectors, there are also malevolent entities believed to roam the Smokies. These spirits are often blamed for unexplained disappearances, mysterious lights, and the eerie feelings experienced by travelers. The Cherokee would perform rituals and ceremonies to appease these spirits, seeking protection and guidance during their journeys through the mountains.

The Legacy of the Spirits

The stories and beliefs surrounding the Cherokee spirits continue to influence the cultural and spiritual landscape of the Great Smoky Mountains. Travelers, hikers, and locals alike share tales of strange occurrences, unexplained sounds, and the feeling of being watched while traversing the dense forests and misty peaks of the Smokies.

For those who tread upon the trails of the Great Smoky Mountains, the whispers of the ancient Cherokee spirits may still be heard. Some hikers report seeing flickering lights in the distance, hearing faint melodies or cries carried by the wind, and experiencing an inexplicable sense of awe and reverence for the land.

The Cherokee spirits of the Great Smoky Mountains represent the intertwining of natural beauty and spiritual mystique, offering a glimpse into the rich history and beliefs of the Native Cherokee people. Whether these tales are seen as mere folklore or as metaphors for the indescribable magic of the Smokies, they continue to captivate the hearts and imaginations of all who venture into these ancient, whispering mountains.

Twelve

TALE OF THE TAILYPO

THE TAILYPO IS a mythical creature deeply embedded in the folklore of the Appalachian region, specifically in the areas surrounding the Appalachian Trail. Although variations of the story exist, the Tailypo legend has been consistently characterized by its haunting narrative and enigmatic creature, casting a spooky ambiance over the Appalachian wilderness.

The Tailypo creature is often described as being similar in size to a dog or a large cat but possesses features unlike any identifiable animal. With elongated, sharp claws and teeth, its physical characteristics are striking and fearsome. Its fur is commonly depicted as dark or black, with glowing red eyes that pierce through the night. However, the most distinctive feature is its long, bushy tail, which plays a central role in the stories recounted about it.

Like many folklore tales, the origin of the Tailypo is somewhat ambiguous, with different communities having variations of the story. Generally, the legend is thought to have been passed down orally among the indigenous tribes of the Appalachian region and later adopted and modified by European settlers. The Tailypo story combines elements of Native American folklore with the settlers' own cultural influences, creating a unique and chilling piece of American mythology.

One of the most common versions of the Tailypo story involves a hermit or an old man living alone in a cabin within the dense Appalachian forests. Facing dire poverty, the man is desperate for food. One night, he encounters the Tailypo creature and, in a bid for survival, manages to cut off its tail. The tail is then cooked and eaten by the man, providing a much-needed source of nourishment.

However, this act incurs the wrath of the Tailypo, initiating a series of terrifying and supernatural events. The creature begins to haunt the old man, its chilling cries of "Tailypo, Tailypo, give me back my Tailypo!" echoing through the dark, silent nights. Despite attempts to ward off or escape from the creature, the old man is eventually confronted by the Tailypo, resulting in his mysterious and ominous disappearance.

Different iterations of the Tailypo story exist, with

variations often reflecting the cultural and geographical nuances of the communities that tell them. In some versions, the old man has dogs that try to protect him from the Tailypo, but they too eventually fall victim to the creature's relentless pursuit. Other versions incorporate elements of dark humor, tragedy, or moral lessons, demonstrating the tale's adaptability and enduring relevance.

The Tailypo legend can be interpreted in several ways. On one level, it serves as a cautionary tale about the consequences of greed and disrespect for the natural world. The old man's desperate act of severing and consuming the Tailypo's tail can be seen as a violation of the delicate balance between humans and nature, resulting in inevitable retribution.

Furthermore, the tale might be viewed as an embodiment of the isolation, fear, and unknown inherent to the vast Appalachian wilderness. The Tailypo creature itself symbolizes the untamed and inscrutable aspects of nature, its presence a constant reminder of the mysteries and dangers lurking within the shadows of the forest.

The Tailypo is more than a mere spooky tale; it is a rich and multifaceted legend that reflects the fears, imagination, and cultural history of the Appalachian people. Its elusive and terrifying creature, haunting cries, and dramatic narrative continue to capture the imagination, making it a beloved and enduring part of American folklore. Whether told around campfires or passed down through generations, the Tale of the Tailypo remains a chilling and fascinating exploration of the unknown, the supernatural, and the inexorable power of nature.

Thirteen

HOOTIN' ANNIE

The mysterious Hootin' Annie occupies a unique and unsettling place. While there are different variations to the legend, the common thread across all stories is the unmistakable haunting cries attributed to Hootin' Annie.

Hootin' Annie is often described as an otherworldly owl-like creature, noted for its distinct and chilling cries that reverberate through the hills and valleys of the Appalachian Mountains. The echoes of Hootin' Annie are said to be ominous and foreboding, often believed to be harbingers of tragedy, misfortune, or death.

Though accounts vary, many describe Hootin' Annie as being an unusually large and imposing owl with supernatural qualities. With eyes that glow menacingly in the darkness and a voice that oscillates between melancholic hoots and sharp, shrieking cries, Hootin' Annie is both fascinating and terrifying. The creature is elusive, often heard but seldom seen, adding to its enigmatic and spectral reputation.

The legend of Hootin' Annie is deeply rooted in the oral traditions of the Appalachian communities. The story seems to draw from a mixture of indigenous folklore and the beliefs of early European settlers in the region. Native American tribes had their own set of beliefs regarding owls, often viewing them as omens or messengers from the spirit world, while European settlers brought with them tales of banshees and other supernatural entities.

Stories about encounters with Hootin' Annie are numerous and varied, often shared and embellished through generations. In many tales, individuals or families hear the cries of Hootin' Annie preceding a significant and usually tragic event. The spectral owl is often spotted or heard near graveyards, abandoned structures, and deep within the forests, further cementing its association with the supernatural and the unknown.

Some narratives also recount personal encounters with Hootin' Annie, where the creature directly interacts with or observes individuals, usually resulting in feelings of intense fear and dread. These stories often serve both as eerie entertainment and cautionary tales warning against disrespecting or challenging the supernatural forces believed to inhabit the Appalachian wilderness.

Hootin' Annie can be interpreted in various ways. For some, the creature symbolizes the unknown and uncontrollable forces of nature and fate. Its cries represent the thin boundary between the living and the dead, the known and the unknown, reflecting the uncertainties and anxieties of life in a wild and unpredictable landscape.

For others, Hootin' Annie serves as a metaphorical embodiment of loss, grief, and impending doom. The haunting cries resonate with the collective fears and sorrows of the community, echoing through the hills as a constant reminder of the fragility and transience of life.

The legend of Hootin' Annie continues to be a significant aspect of Appalachian folklore and cultural identity. Its tales are shared amongst locals and visitors alike, often recounted during gatherings, camping trips, or quiet nights by the fire. The haunting cries attributed to Hootin' Annie, whether real or imagined, continue to inspire awe, fear, and fascination, contributing to the rich and mysterious tapestry of stories and legends that define the Appalachian region.

Enigmatic and chilling, the legend of Hootin' Annie is a captivating tale that reflects the complex interplay between nature, superstition, and the human psyche. Its haunting cries, whether borne out of the imagination of a people closely tied to their environment or echoing truthfully through the misty Appalachian nights, remain an indelible part of the region's folklore, whispered and wondered about as the sun sets behind the imposing mountain range.

Fourteen

LUCY OF ROARING FORK

WITHIN THE SERENE, picturesque landscapes of Roaring Fork, nestled deep within the Great Smoky Mountains, whispers of a spectral presence named "Lucy" have long circulated amongst locals and visitors alike. Lucy is envisioned as a ghostly figure, a relic of a time long past, eternally wandering the meandering trails and haunting the dense, mist-enshrouded forests of Roaring Fork.

The legend of Lucy is not precisely dated but is steeped in the rich tapestry of local folklore. Lucy is said to have lived in the area in the late 1800s or early 1900s. The most popular rendition of the tale describes her as a young woman of striking beauty and indomitable spirit, living in a small cabin within the woods.

One fateful day, as the story goes, a severe and sudden storm swept through the mountains, bringing with it torrential rains and chilling winds. Lucy, who had ventured out into the woods, found herself caught amidst this furious onslaught of nature. Despite her attempts to seek refuge, she succumbed to the elements, her life tragically and prematurely extinguished.

Since that tragic event, there have been numerous reported sightings and encounters with Lucy's spirit in the Roaring Fork area. Hikers and travelers have shared chilling tales of a translucent figure, often spotted at dusk or dawn, wandering through the woods with a melancholic expression etched on her visage. The apparition is often described as wearing period clothing, further accentuating the legend's historical roots.

The air around Roaring Fork is said to crackle with an unspoken energy on certain nights, with the soft, lilting sound of a woman's voice weaving through the trees. Some have reported hearing faint sobs, echoing through the otherwise tranquil wilderness, heightening the sense of mystery and otherworldliness enveloping the area.

Lucy's cabin, though now in ruins, is believed to be located off the beaten path, hidden amongst the overgrown vegetation and towering trees. The cabin is frequently mentioned in the tales, described as an inexplicably preserved space where time appears to stand still. Those who claimed to have stumbled upon it describe an eerie sensation of being watched and a palpable sadness permeating the air.

The legend of Lucy, while captivating, resides in the realm of folklore and the supernatural, with no concrete evidence to validate the tales spun around her existence. The stories have been passed down through generations, morphing and evolving with each telling. Whether Lucy truly existed or is a manifestation of the area's haunting beauty and inherent danger remains uncertain.

Lucy of Roaring Fork continues to be a prominent figure in the local folklore of the Great Smoky Mountains, her tragic tale encapsulating the allure and peril of the wild, untamed beauty of the region. For those navigating the dense woods and rugged trails of Roaring Fork, the legend of Lucy serves as both a poignant reminder of the past and a chilling tale that adds an extra layer of mystique to the mesmerizing landscapes. Whether folklore or truth, the legend of Lucy undoubtedly contributes to the enigmatic allure that continues to draw individuals to explore the secrets hidden within the shadows of the Smokies.

Fifteen

MOTHMAN

THE LEGEND OF THE MOTHMAN, a creature deeply entrenched within American paranormal folklore, is primarily associated with the town of Point Pleasant in West Virginia. However, whispers and tales have spread along the Appalachian Trail, with several claimed sightings of a similar ominous entity, casting a cryptic aura over this renowned hiking route.

According to accounts, the Mothman along the Appalachian Trail is described as a large, humanoid figure with glowing red eyes and enormous wings that allow it to soar through the night sky. Hikers and campers who have allegedly encountered the Mothman describe a feeling of impending doom, a sensation that is often reported in the more famous sightings in Point Pleasant.

Various alleged sightings have trickled in over the years,

often from hikers or locals living near the trail. While details differ, the common thread among these stories is the sighting of a flying creature with human features, causing an inexplicable sense of dread among those who encounter it.

Some reports include hikers waking up to the sounds of heavy flapping, only to see a large shadow fleeting above their campsites under the moonlight. Others have mentioned discovering mutilated wildlife, a phenomenon that some attribute to the mythical creature.

Tales of the Mothman along the Appalachian Trail have become cautionary tales among the hiking community. The sightings are often used to emphasize the unknown dangers of the wilderness and the importance of being vigilant when traversing the remote and unforgiving terrains along the trail.

Despite the numerous stories and accounts, there's considerable skepticism regarding the existence of the Mothman on the Appalachian Trail. Critics argue that these tales are likely the result of misidentification of large birds or nocturnal animals, possibly owls or bats, coupled with the suggestive power of the famous Mothman legend.

The Mothman sightings contribute to the rich tapestry of folklore and myth that surrounds the Appalachian Trail. These tales, whether believed or dismissed, add an element of mystique to the trail, captivating the imaginations of those who hike and treasure the path. For some, the Mothman represents the unknown and unexplainable aspects of the natural world, embodying the fears and fascinations humans harbor toward the wilderness.

Whether a myth born out of fear and the unknown or a real entity lurking in the shadows of the Appalachian woods, the Mothman remains a compelling part of the trail's folklore. Stories of its sightings continue to be shared around campfires, casting an eerie glow on the faces of listeners and infusing the night air with a sense of mystery and apprehension. As long as the Appalachian Trail winds through the hills and valleys, tales like that of the Mothman will continue to haunt, fascinate, and warn those who dare to walk its storied path.

Sixteen

BIGFOOT

THE APPALACHIAN TRAIL, with its expansive forests and secluded spaces, has long been a canvas for legends and folklore. Among these, the tales of Bigfoot, or Sasquatch, stand out, capturing the imaginations of hikers, locals, and cryptozoologists alike.

Bigfoot is often described as a large, hairy, ape-like creature, walking upright and possessing enormous strength. Sightings along the Appalachian Trail depict the creature as elusive, often appearing at dusk or dawn, vanishing into the thick woods before observers can get a clear look.

The history of Bigfoot sightings along the Appalachian Trail can be traced back centuries, with indigenous tribes having their own lore about wild, giant men living in the depths of the forests. These early tales set the stage for the modern Bigfoot mythos, intertwining with the oral histories and traditions of the local communities.

In recent years, hikers and adventurers have reported numerous sightings and encounters with creatures resembling Bigfoot along various sections of the Appalachian Trail. These accounts often include finding large, unexplained footprints, hearing strange, powerful howls at night, and spotting tall, shadowy figures moving swiftly through the trees.

Sighting Report:

"I always knew bigfoot existed or at the very least I always believed that it did. Just like so many other people who eventually went on to have their own encounters, I spent most of my life in the woods of Maine where I grew up and heard all the legends of the "man ape" that was said to lurk around in them. I don't think anyone back then, in the sixties, had any idea the scope of what th3e legend entailed or would go on to become. We all thought it was just one thing and even after my encounter and up until recently that's what I thought too. We all know about bigfoot now, or at least it stands to reason if you're reading this encounter you've at the very least heard of it. I refer to the creature as it and not as him because I not only figure there has to be a female of the species for them to reproduce but also because I am certain I saw one that was female. Of course, there's no real way of knowing but I am pretty sure of that fact. My encounter happened in 1967 when I was twenty-two years old. I'm an old man now and though much of my memories have escaped me at this point, that's not what happened with the bigfoot memory. In fact, it's just as clear in my mind as though I had just seen it yesterday. I don't have dementia, I'm just old and I didn't drink to excess or do drugs in my lifetime. I wasn't drinking at all at the time of my encounter because I was out day hiking by myself and had to be my own designated driver. It was in the woods of northern Maine, and I was heading on a very average day trip, and it was something I did at least once a week by myself and sometimes more often than that if weather permitted and my bust schedule at the time allowed. I hadn't ever actually seen anything out of the ordinary up to that point, but I had heard some strange stuff and had gotten some weird feelings sometimes while I was out there too.

I went to a local camping area near the Appalachian Trail and paid to park for the day. I had twelve hours before my ticket ran out, but I knew it would only take me about eight hours to hike up the trail I wanted to hike up and back to the parking lot. It started off as usual and it wasn't until about an hour into my hike, after I had decided to take a different trail than the one, I had taken all the other times I had hiked in that spot, and I came across a small lake. I knew there were several water sources in that part of the forest, and I wasn't exactly right on the Appalachian Trail, but I was very near to it. I had come across one other small body of water a year or two before, but I had been hiking then in the winter and I couldn't go into the water then. It was a beautiful and clear summer day, in the middle of July and I decided it would be a good idea to take a quick dip in the lake. There were signs posted telling anyone who passed by that when they swam there, they did so at their own risk, but I was young and thought I knew everything. I walked to the shore and laid my pack down. I had a book with me because I always stopped for an hour and had a little picnic lunch and so I set everything up there and sat out reading my book and eating some of the food I had brought with me. I left the food out on the blanket, what was left of it anyway, and figured I would just clean it all up once I got done with my quick swim. I ran over to the water and walked right in. I went under the water and when I came up, everything looked perfectly normal at first. After a few minutes though I started to get the sense that I was being watched and that whatever was watching me was doing so from the woods beyond where my picnic was still sitting. I immediately thought that maybe some wild and predatory animal had smelled the meat on my sandwiches or something like that and so I got out of the water to clean all of it up, figuring I would go back in for a few more minutes before heading out on my way.

I got out of the water and as soon as I did, I heard a very strange hollering sound echoing across the water, coming from the other side of the lake. It was about a hundred yards or so away, but I could hear whatever it was as though it were right next to me. It was a noise I had never heard before which was odd because as I already said I grew up hanging around in the woods and spent most of my time in them. Also, I had been hiking in that forest for at least four years at that point, every single week in the summertime and once a month in the winter and had never heard anything as aggressive sounding, somewhat pathetic and loud. It sounded like it was whining, whatever it was, but it also sounded angry. I know that may not make much sense to many of you reading this but that's the best way that I can think of to describe what I was hearing. It scared me, that's for sure, but it didn't deter me from going back into the water. Instead, I cleaned up and then sat there, as though I were reading my book again, but looking out into that area of the woods in order to see if anything would present itself so I could figure out exactly what I was dealing with and whether or not it was something I should get far away from very quickly or something that I could ignore that would ignore me. It took about five minutes for the creature to come out of the woods. I grabbed my binoculars and couldn't believe what I saw.

It was some sort of man ape but it had women's breasts. I can't find much online even nowadays about female bigfoot, but I still believe I saw one. I have seen many encounters where someone believes they saw a family of bigfoot but the only distinction they make between the males and females are the size, with the female being smaller. However, I know what I saw, and I also know it deep down in my guts that that's what it was. The creature was about nine feet tall and was covered head to toe with black hair. Unlike most people who believe they've encountered bigfoot too, this one didn't have dirty looking, mangy, or matted fur. It looked clean and almost bright. The sun somewhat shimmered off it. It seemed to be unaware of me at first although I knew that more than likely that wasn't the case because it was just hollering a few moments earlier and I hadn't gone anywhere where it wouldn't have been able to see me. Also, it seemed to be looking everywhere except at me and something inside of me felt like it was doing that on purpose. The creature stood there with the water about up to its waist for a good ten minutes as I watched it through my binoculars and then suddenly, without warning, it dove headfirst into the water. Its arms were by its sides when it did so, and I figured it would come right back up. I mean, it was obvious to me that it had been some sort of mammal or something similar and so I figured it would have needed to come up for some air. That's what I figured anyway, but that ended up not seeming to be the case. I sat there for at least fifteen minutes waiting to see if it would come up from the water for air and it never did. I had good binoculars and in fact they were the best ones you could have at the time, and I looked all around the lake. I also took the time to walk around the lake to see if there were any wet footprints, either leading back into the woods or otherwise, but there was no sign at all that the bigfoot had been there. I was shocked but more, so I was scared. It was unheard of to have conversations about the paranormal or to mention seeing a bigfoot in public, even to your friends. Also, even having a private conversation with a family member or friend about something like that could have been dangerous to someone's reputation or livelihood etc. So, I kept it to myself.

I hightailed it out of there and didn't even mention the encounter to my closest friends, including those who themselves had many conversations around the bonfires and while camping about the "ape man" in the woods of Maine. I started talking about it in the late seventies when it was somewhat cool to be weird and being weird meant discussing the paranormal, which at the time is what we all thought bigfoot was. Nowadays we understand that it is some sort of cryptid or, and it varies greatly depending on who you ask but these are the two main theories I hear repeatedly, some sort of beast in the woods that has regular origins but just hasn't been "discovered" yet. I feel like it being something perfectly natural and something we merely haven't discovered and named yet, here in 2023, has about as much likelihood of being the case as hell freezing over. That's just me though and I don't judge other people's opinions or theories because I firmly believe that our life experiences shape what those are and that, for the most part at least, they evolve throughout our lives. I never had any other encounters with bigfoot, and I wish I hadn't been so scared back then because I would have gone into the water and tried to find it if it happened in a time when it was socially acceptable to see what I saw. My story doesn't completely end there though so let me tell you all about my hike back down the trail and to my car.

I ended up leaving right after the encounter and didn't even finish the hike I had originally planned for that day. I was kicking myself for going off the trail and onto another one that was unfamiliar to me. I felt the whole time like I was being watched and something in the darkest depths of my mind kept telling me to just look up. I had no intention of looking up or doing any such thing and never did the whole way back. I knew somehow that there was at least one bigfoot creature up in those trees and the noises I heard the whole way back down that trail was the bigfoot jumping through the air from tree to tree, way up high in the trees themselves. It was leaping! I didn't want to see anymore, and I knew I also didn't want to know anymore. The person collecting the money asked me if I was okay, mainly due to the fact I was back and done with my hike so quickly and so early and told me I looked as though I had just seen a ghost. I mumbled and sputtered something out about having a stomach bug and shakily ran to my vehicle to get the hell out of there. I didn't go back to that spot until about fifteen years later and when I did go back then, I took several friends with me and told them what I was looking for out there. We camped for the entire weekend at that lake but never saw, heard, or even felt a thing. I found out from the guy who took the parking money that the particular lake we had told him we would be spending the night at was one hundred and fifty feet deep in the middle of it so that also makes me wonder if perhaps there is something there, down at the bottom of it, that no one has ever thought to try and discover or explore. In 1982 that lake was walled off and there were signs that warned people to stay out, that it was unsafe, and trespassers would be prosecuted and fined. We were even told we could get jail time. I often wonder if maybe someone did find something out about what lurked not only in the woods surrounding that lake but in the depths of it itself. That's something I guess I will never know, and my physical health has declined enough that I haven't been able to walk in ten years so hiking or trying to hop a wall to get some answers is completely out of the question. Thanks for letting me share this and I hope it helps someone else who has perhaps had a similarly scary or strange experience and is afraid to come forward and talk about it to do so.

Despite the numerous accounts, there is considerable skepticism regarding Bigfoot's existence. Critics argue that the sightings are either hoaxes, misidentifications of wildlife, or the product of overactive imaginations. Without tangible evidence, the Bigfoot legends remain in the realm of folklore and speculation.

The Bigfoot legends have ingrained themselves into the cultural fabric of the Appalachian Trail. They inspire curiosity and wonder, contributing to the trail's mystical and untamed image. Books, documentaries, and even festivals celebrate the elusive creature, showcasing the human fascination with the unknown.

Whether real or imagined, the tales of Bigfoot along the Appalachian Trail continue to thrill and mystify. These stories, whispered around campfires and shared between hikers, add an extra layer of magic and mystery to the already enchanting landscape of the trail. Until definitive evidence is found, Bigfoot will remain a shadowy giant lurking in the tales and legends of the Appalachian wilderness, ever elusive and endlessly captivating.

Seventeen

SERIAL KILLERS ON THE TRAIL

Gary Hilton - The Appalachian Trail Predator

Gary Michael Hilton, known for his heinous crimes along the Appalachian Trail, etched a dark legacy in the early 2000s. His series of murders in the picturesque but remote wilderness sowed fear among hikers and residents in the surrounding areas. This chapter aims to delve into the life, crimes, and eventual downfall of Hilton, illuminating the shadows cast by this notorious figure.

Gary Hilton was born in November 1946. Details about his early life are sparse, but it's understood that he had a tumultuous relationship with his family and struggled socially. He served in the military during the Vietnam War, but his service was marked by disciplinary issues.

Hilton's criminal activities escalated over time. Initially involved in petty crimes, he gradually descended into more violent offenses. He was known to be a drifter, spending extensive time in the natural reserves and mountainous terrains of the Appalachian region.

One of Hilton's most infamous crimes was the kidnapping and murder of Meredith Emerson, a 24-year-old hiker, in January 2008. Emerson was hiking with her dog on Georgia's Blood Mountain when she encountered Hilton. Witnesses last saw her in his company. After a meticulous search, Emerson's decapitated body was found, leading to Hilton's arrest. He eventually pleaded guilty to her murder and provided details about the crime, resulting in a life sentence.

Emerson was not Hilton's only victim. Authorities linked him to the murder of an elderly couple, John and Irene Bryant, who were hiking in North Carolina. Hilton was also implicated in the killing of Cheryl Dunlap in Florida. Each crime exhibited a chilling modus operandi, where the victims were abducted, tormented, and eventually killed.

Hilton's reign of terror ended with his arrest and subsequent conviction. He was sentenced to life in prison for Emerson's murder, and he received a death sentence in Florida for Dunlap's murder. His crimes sent shockwaves through the community, prompting discussions and initiatives to enhance safety measures in hiking trails and wilderness areas.

Gary Hilton's crimes left an indelible mark on the Appalachian Trail community. His acts cast shadows over the pristine wilderness, turning the serene trails into haunting landscapes for those who remembered the tales of the Appalachian Trail Predator. In the wake of his crimes, hikers and authorities alike became more vigilant, working to ensure that the trails remained safe for all.

The Dark Journey of Randall Lee Smith

Randall Lee Smith, whose name has been etched into the sinister annals of Appalachian Trail history, was involved in a series of heinous crimes that sent shockwaves through the hiking community. His dark tale begins in 1981 when the Appalachian Trail witnessed a tragic event that would forever taint its serene wilderness.

Little is known about Randall Lee Smith's early life, as he primarily became known for the criminal activities he later engaged in. Smith was a local of Pearisburg, Virginia, living near the tranquil but treacherous terrains of the Appalachian Trail.

In May 1981, the peaceful aura of the Appalachian Trail was shattered when two hikers, Susan Ramsey and Robert Mountford Jr., were found dead near the trail in Virginia. Both had been shot and their bodies left in the dense, secluded woods, creating an atmosphere of dread and horror amongst other hikers and local residents.

Ramsey and Mountford were actively involved in social work and were trekking the trail to raise funds for a Maine special education school. Their journey, filled with hope and benevolence, met a tragic end at the hands of Smith.

Following the discovery of the bodies, an extensive investigation was launched, leading to the arrest of Randall Lee Smith. Despite the absence of a clear motive, evidence against Smith was overwhelming, resulting in his conviction. The courts sentenced him to two consecutive life sentences, but an appeal would later reduce his incarceration period.

Smith was released on parole in 1996, having served merely 15 years of his sentence. Shockingly, he would return to a life of crime, his freedom leading to another gruesome incident near the Appalachian Trail in 2008.

Smith attacked two fishermen, Scott Johnston and Sean Farmer, near the trail close to where he had committed the first set of murders. Although injured, Johnston and Farmer managed to escape, and Smith was soon apprehended by the authorities. However, fate had its own plans, as Smith died in custody, succumbing to injuries sustained during a vehicle crash while he was attempting to elude capture.

Randall Lee Smith's crimes cast a long shadow over the Appalachian Trail community, sowing seeds of fear and caution amongst those who sought solace in its serene embrace. His tale serves as a chilling reminder that danger can lurk even in the most unexpected and tranquil places.

His actions, while horrifying, are anomalies amidst the myriad of inspiring and uplifting stories that have originated from the trail over the years. The Appalachian Trail, with its majestic landscapes and the promise of adventure, continues to beckon to those seeking connection with nature and themselves, albeit with the cautionary tales of the past echoing through its misty, silent woods.

Shadows on the Trail: Paul David Crews

In the quiet, serene landscapes of the Appalachian Trail, where nature unveils its raw beauty, there lurk tales of shadowy figures that have, over time, painted certain sections of the trail with strokes of dread and fear. One such figure that haunts the annals of the trail's history is Paul David Crews, a name synonymous with a chilling double murder that unfolded in the summer of 1990.

Little is publicly known about the early life of Paul David Crews due to the limited availability of records. It is known that he hailed from Florida and had a troubled background, with various run-ins with the law. Crews was somewhat of a drifter, and by the time he reached Pennsylvania, he had a criminal record and was wanted for parole violations.

In September 1990, two hikers, Molly LaRue and Geoffrey Hood, were traversing the picturesque but challenging terrains of the Appalachian Trail. LaRue, originally from Shaker Heights, Ohio, and Hood, from Signal Mountain, Tennessee, were experienced and enthusiastic outdoor adventurers. However, the duo's fateful encounter with Crews at the Thelma Marks Shelter near Duncannon, Pennsylvania, would bring their journey to a tragic end.

LaRue and Hood were part of a community of hikers that shared a passion for exploration and adventure. They had formed bonds with fellow travelers and were well-known and respected in the hiker community. Unfortunately, their paths crossed with Crews, who, bearing a shotgun, embodied danger and malice.

On the tragic day, Crews attacked and killed Hood, shooting him in the back with his shotgun. The motive of the attack remains uncertain, though it's speculated that robbery and Crews' unstable mental state played significant roles. After killing Hood, Crews proceeded to attack LaRue, binding her hands and killing her. The bodies of the two hikers were later found at the shelter.

The double homicide sent shockwaves through the hiker community and law enforcement agencies engaged in a manhunt to capture Crews. He was eventually apprehended while attempting to flee and was charged with the heinous crimes.

During the trial, Crews was found guilty of the murders and was sentenced to life in prison without the possibility of parole. The judgment brought some semblance of closure to the families of the victims, but the echoes of the tragedy continued to reverberate through the Appalachian Trail community.

The murders committed by Paul David Crews added a dark chapter to the history of the Appalachian Trail. This event served as a harsh reminder of the vulnerabilities hikers might face on the trail, prompting discussions and measures to improve safety for those seeking solitude and adventure in the wilderness.

The tale of Paul David Crews and the tragic events of 1990 at the Thelma Marks Shelter remain etched in the collective memory of the Appalachian Trail community. These events, while casting a long shadow, also highlight the resilience and strength of the hiker community, serving as a somber reminder to tread lightly and stay vigilant while embracing the call of the wild. The trail, with its undulating hills, dense forests, and breathtaking vistas, continues to inspire and beckon adventurers, while silently bearing witness to tales of joy, discovery, and loss.

Terror on the Trail: James Jordan

James Louis Jordan, an individual known to many on the Appalachian Trail as "Sovereign," cast a dark shadow on the iconic hiking route in 2019. His actions left the tight-knit community of trail enthusiasts shaken, highlighting the unpredictable dangers that might lurk in the most unexpected places.

Limited information is available on Jordan's early life, and much of what is known emerges from the period leading up to and during his crimes on the Appalachian Trail. It's crucial to approach such profiles with the understanding that the information might not provide a comprehensive view of the individual's life history.

James Jordan began appearing on the Appalachian Trail in early 2019. Fellow hikers and trail enthusiasts noticed his erratic and often intimidating behavior. He was known to approach camping groups menacingly, sometimes brandishing a knife, leading to several uncomfortable and threatening encounters.

Jordan was initially arrested in April 2019 after an altercation with fellow hikers on the trail. However, he was eventually released with probation, allowing him to return to the trail. The early incidents with Jordan set a tense atmosphere among hikers, leading many to share warnings and advice on how to avoid or handle encounters with him.

In May 2019, the tensions culminated in a tragic incident near the Wythe County portion of the trail in Virginia. Jordan attacked a group of four hikers camping together for safety. He approached their camp singing and playing his guitar before threatening them. In the ensuing struggle, one hiker was injured, and another, Ronald S. Sanchez Jr., a U.S. Army veteran, was fatally stabbed.

The other hikers managed to escape, alerting authorities to the dangerous situation unfolding on the trail. It led to a swift response, with law enforcement agencies mobilizing to locate and apprehend Jordan.

James Jordan was arrested and charged with murder and assault with the intent to murder. The event sent shockwaves through the Appalachian Trail community, highlighting the unpredictability of the dangers hikers might face even from fellow travelers.

The incident prompted discussions and reflections on safety, preparedness, and community among hikers. The tragic loss of Ronald Sanchez and the terror experienced by others in the group served as a sobering reminder of the importance of vigilance and support within the hiking community.

Jordan was deemed competent to stand trial after a psychiatric evaluation, though proceedings have been delayed and drawn out. The case brought against him underscores the delicate balance between addressing mental health issues and ensuring that justice is served for the victims and their families.

The shadow cast by James Jordan on the Appalachian Trail in 2019 is a dark chapter in the history of this beloved hiking route. The events serve as a tragic reminder of the unpredictability of life and the importance of community, vigilance, and preparedness when venturing into the wilderness. As the legal proceedings against Jordan continue, the hiking community remembers, reflects, and learns from the incidents, hoping to prevent similar tragedies in the future.

The stories of these four killers underscores the necessity of vigilance and preparedness when embarking on adventures in isolated areas like the Appalachian Trail. Be safe out there and maintain situational awareness at all times.

MISSING PEOPLE CASES

OVER THE YEARS, several hikers and individuals have gone missing while venturing on or around the Appalachian Trail. While many missing persons cases are eventually resolved as lost hikers are found or their fates are discovered, others remain shrouded in mystery, contributing to the trail's lore and history. Below are some of the most well-known or intriguing cases.

Vanishing Echoes: The Dennis Lloyd Martin Disappearance

In the annals of Appalachian mysteries, few are as enduring and heartbreaking as the disappearance of Dennis Lloyd Martin. In 1969, the six-year-old vanished without a trace from the Great Smoky Mountains National Park, leaving behind a trail of questions and a legacy of sorrow.

June 14, 1969, started as a joyous day for the Martin family. On a camping trip in the Smokies, the family decided to hike up to Spence Field, a popular meadow along the Appalachian Trail, near the border between North Carolina and Tennessee. Upon reaching the destination, Dennis and his brother, along with some other children, decided to play a prank on the adults by jumping out of the bushes to surprise them.

The boys were supposed to jump out of the bushes simultaneously to surprise the adults. While the other boys executed the plan, Dennis, who had been seen going behind a bush, did not reappear. This marked the last time anyone saw him. Despite wearing a highly visible, bright red shirt, he seemed to have vanished into thin air.

Dennis's father, William Martin, immediately sprung into action, searching a two-mile radius around Spence Field but to no avail. Soon after, the National Park Service was notified, and one of the most extensive search-and-rescue missions in the history of the southeastern United States began.

The search for Dennis was plagued by a series of challenges. Heavy rains fell in the area soon after his disappearance, washing away potential tracks and clues.

Additionally, there were communication issues and coordination problems among the different agencies and hundreds of volunteers involved in the search.

During the search, a family reported hearing a child's scream and later finding shoe prints consistent with a boy's Oxford-style shoe, which Dennis was wearing. Unfortunately, this lead was not immediately followed up on, leading to speculation and controversy regarding the investigation's handling.

Over the years, theories about Dennis's disappearance have proliferated. Some believe he was abducted; others think he succumbed to the elements, while others speculate about wild animal attacks.

The disappearance of Dennis Lloyd Martin has left an indelible mark on the Great Smoky Mountains National Park and the broader Appalachian community. The case has spawned countless articles, documentaries, and book chapters, serving as a chilling reminder of the wilderness's unpredictability and danger.

Despite the passage of over five decades, the mystery of Dennis Lloyd Martin's disappearance remains unsolved, casting a long, enigmatic shadow over the Smokies. The story continues to evoke a sense of loss and caution in those who venture into the vast, beautiful, and sometimes unforgiving expanse of the Appalachian wilderness. Each retelling of the tale serves not only as a eulogy for a life lost too soon but also as a solemn reminder to respect and navigate carefully through nature's mesmerizing but perilous terrains.

* * *

Vanished in the Vales: The Disappearance of Thelma Pauline Melton

In the realm of mysterious disappearances along the Appalachian Trail, the case of Thelma Pauline Melton, affectionately known as "Polly," stands out as one of the most haunting and puzzling. The story of her disappearance in 1981 remains etched in the collective memory of the hiking community and those familiar with the Great Smoky Mountains National Park.

At the age of 58, Thelma Pauline Melton was an experienced hiker, intimately acquainted with the undulating trails and picturesque vistas of the Smokies. She often retreated to the embrace of these ancient hills, seeking solace and rejuvenation amidst their silent strength and timeless beauty.

On September 25, 1981, Polly set out with friends on what was supposed to be a serene and invigorating hike near the Appalachian Trail in the Deep Creek area of the park. Engulfed by a canvas of lush greenery and accompanied by the melodic whispers of the creek, the group of friends was unaware that the day would unfold into a haunting tale of mystery and loss.

Polly was walking ahead of her two friends, and as the trail unfolded, she moved out of their sight. It was the last time her companions, and indeed anyone, would see her. When her friends arrived at the designated meeting point, Polly was nowhere to be found. The tranquil ambiance of the park swiftly transformed into an ominous silence, heavy with the weight of the unknown.

The news of Polly's disappearance sent shockwaves through the community, prompting an immediate and extensive search. Hundreds of volunteers, park rangers, and law enforcement personnel combed through the rugged terrain, plunging into the dense foliage and navigating the treacherous landscape in a race against time.

Despite the exhaustive efforts and the eyes meticulously scanning every inch of the area, no trace of Polly was found. The search expanded, covering a broad swath of land, but the Smokies remained silent, guarding their secrets with stoic resolve.

In the wake of Polly's disappearance, various theories and speculations swirled around, attempting to make sense of the inexplicable. Some believed she might have lost her footing and fallen into a concealed ravine or crevice, while others speculated about possible foul play. However, with no evidence or leads emerging, the case gradually grew cold, leaving a void filled by whispers, stories, and the undying hope for closure.

Polly's disappearance remains one of the many mysteries that cloak the Appalachian Trail and the Smokies. Over the years, her story has been revisited by journalists, investigators, and those intrigued by unsolved cases. Yet, the answers remain elusive, tucked away in the silent heart of the mountains.

For those who tread upon the trails that Polly once walked, her story serves as a sobering reminder of the unpredictability and inherent dangers of the wild. It's a tale whispered through the rustling leaves and echoed in the murmuring creeks, a silent hymn to the enigmatic and indomitable spirit of the Appalachian wilderness.

The disappearance of Thelma Pauline Melton is a haunting narrative that continues to reverberate through the corridors of time. It's a poignant reminder of the mysteries that unfold in the shadows of nature's grandeur, the tales spun in the silence of the forests, and the echoes of the lost that blend with the eternal symphony of the wild. Each step on the Appalachian Trail whispers these stories, inviting those who listen to reflect, remember, and tread lightly upon the sacred tapestry of earth and sky.

* * *

Lost in the Wilderness: The Geraldine Largay Story
Introduction

Geraldine Largay, affectionately known as "Gerry" to friends and "Inchworm" to her fellow hikers, was a 66-year-old experienced hiker from Tennessee who met a tragic fate on the Appalachian Trail in 2013. Her disappearance and the subsequent discovery of her remains are sober reminders of the unpredictable nature of wilderness adventures.

Geraldine began her thru-hike of the Appalachian Trail in April 2013 with a close friend. They planned to traverse the approximately 2,200-mile-long trail from Georgia to Maine together. However, due to a family emergency, her companion had to leave the hike in June. Despite this, Geraldine decided to continue the journey solo, a decision that was supported by her husband, who would meet her at different sections of the trail to resupply.

On July 22, 2013, Geraldine sent a text to her husband, informing him of her plans to meet him in the town of Stratton, Maine, in a couple of days. This was the last communication anyone received from her. When she failed to appear at the designated location, concerns for her safety grew, initiating a massive search operation.

The search for Geraldine Largay was one of the largest in the history of the state of Maine. It involved multiple agencies, including the Maine Warden Service, the FBI, and numerous volunteers. Despite the extensive efforts, the search teams were unable to locate her, and as days turned into weeks and then months, hope of finding her alive dwindled.

Almost two years after her disappearance, on October 14, 2015, a surveyor working for the U.S. Navy found Geraldine's remains more than two miles away from the trail in a dense, wooded area. Her campsite indicated that she had survived for weeks after getting lost. Her journal entries, found at the site, revealed that she tried to reach her husband via text messages but without success due to the lack of cellular reception.

The discovery of Geraldine's remains brought a tragic conclusion to the mystery of her disappearance. The story highlighted the risks associated with solo hiking and the challenges of navigating the dense and often confusing terrain of the Appalachian Trail. Geraldine's fate is a stark reminder for all wilderness enthusiasts to take precautions, plan carefully, and always be prepared for the uncertainties of nature.

Geraldine Largay's story has since served as a cautionary tale within the hiking and outdoor adventure communities. It underscores the importance of preparation, the understanding of navigation tools, and the awareness of the environment in which one is traveling. Her journey and tragic end continue to resonate with those who tread the paths of the Appalachian Trail, serving as silent testimony to the awe-inspiring yet unforgiving wilderness that adventurers navigate.

The story of Geraldine "Inchworm" Largay is one of inspiration, adventure, and tragedy interwoven. While her spirit and passion for hiking continue to inspire, her unfortunate demise stands as a somber reminder of the respect and preparedness that the great outdoors demands. As hikers continue to traverse the undulating terrains and misty peaks of the Appalachian Trail, the tale of Geraldine Largay whispers through the trees, urging caution and reverence for the wild, unpredictable beauty of nature.

The Unseen Departure: Michael Hearon (2008)

Michael Hearon, whose disappearance in 2008 near the Appalachian Trail remains unresolved, has since been embedded in the complex tapestry of mysterious occurrences associated with the Great Smoky Mountains. This chapter seeks to shed light on the known details of his case, acknowledging the pain and uncertainty experienced by his family and friends.

Michael Hearon was a 51-year-old man from Blount County, Tennessee, known for his affable nature and familiarity with the local terrains. An avid outdoorsman, Hearon was accustomed to the challenging landscapes of the Appalachian region.

On August 23, 2008, Hearon reportedly left his home, driving his 2004 Jeep Wrangler. He was headed towards his family's property in the Happy Valley area, a region near the Great Smoky Mountains National Park. Michael was wearing a black t-shirt, blue jeans, and tennis shoes. After he failed to return home, a search commenced to locate him, unfolding into a saga of mystery and uncertainty.

Hearon's Jeep was discovered on his family's property, with no signs of struggle or foul play. The vehicle was parked properly, and his keys were missing. It appeared as though Hearon had arrived at his destination but subsequently vanished without a trace.

Upon discovering the vehicle, local law enforcement and search-and-rescue teams initiated a comprehensive search operation. The extensive effort involved ground searches, canine units, and aerial surveys of the densely wooded area. Despite the meticulous and thorough search spanning weeks, no conclusive evidence or traces of Hearon were found, deepening the enigma of his disappearance.

In the wake of the unsuccessful search, various theories and speculations emerged. Some believed Hearon might have encountered a dangerous animal or fell victim to the treacherous terrains, while others considered the possibility of amnesia or intentional disappearance. However, without concrete evidence, all these remained mere speculations, leaving the case shrouded in uncertainty.

Michael Hearon's disappearance had a profound impact on his family and the local community. The lack of closure and answers left a void, with family members grappling with the unknown fate of their loved one. Over the years, the case has periodically resurfaced in local media, often reigniting interest and discussion among those familiar with the region and its mysteries.

The tale of Michael Hearon is a somber reminder of the mysteries held within the embrace of the majestic, yet unforgiving, Appalachian landscape. For the most accurate and current information, please refer to the latest resources and investigation updates.

Conclusion

As we gently tread the final pages of *Legends and Stories: From the Appalachian Trail*, a whispered silence envelopes the haunting, verdant paths we've traversed together, leaving echoes of tales both old and new reverberating through the ancient forests. The Appalachian Trail, with its breathtaking vistas and shadowy valleys, has been our silent companion through each legend, bearing witness to the stories unfolding under its timeless gaze.

In the tapestry of tales woven from the ethereal threads of history and imagination, the trail stands not just as a mere backdrop but as a character itself, breathing life into the myths that dance like elusive shadows under its sprawling canopy. It's a living, whispering entity, absorbing the footprints and whispers of the countless souls navigating its labyrinthine passages, adding their own stories to its secret vault.

Through the journey within these pages, we encountered whispers of ghostly apparitions flickering at the periphery of vision, tales of elusive creatures that shy away from prying eyes, and sagas inked in the annals of folklore. Every rustling leaf, every silent hill, and each hidden lake along the trail has cradled a story, nestling it within its bosom until the time is ripe for it to be unearthed and retold.

As we bid farewell let the allure of the Appalachian Trail linger in your consciousness, like a soft melody humming through the twilight. The stories unfurling along its expanse are ever-evolving, written and rewritten with each dawn that kisses its soil, awaiting eager ears and open hearts to receive them.

We invite you, dear reader, to not let this conclusion be an end but a portal to your own adventure. May the tales herein inspire you to tread your path along the storied trail, to listen to its silent whispers, and to contribute your own legend to its ever-growing repository. For in the dance between reality and fantasy, between the known and the unknown, there lies magic awaiting discovery, stories begging to be told, and a trail forever winding through the canvas of the wild, beckoning to all who seek the extraordinary within the folds of the earth.

Until we meet again under the sprawling arches of ancient trees, let the *Legends and Stories: From the Appalachian Trail* be your compass guiding you to unseen wonders and unheard tales, illuminating the path with the soft glow of mystery and enchantment that resides within and around us all. Safe travels, and may your steps be light and your heart open to the infinite possibilities whispering through the leaves.

- Steve Stockton

* * *

CONTINUE WITH
LEGENDS AND STORIES: FROM THE PACIFIC
CREST TRAIL

About the Author

Steve Stockton is a veteran outdoorsman and author who has been investigating the unexplained for over 35 years. Originally from the mountains of East Tennessee, Steve has traveled all over the country and many parts of the world and now makes his home in picturesque New England with his wife, Nicole, and their dog, Mulder.

Steve cites his influences as his "gypsy witch" grandmother, who told him multitudes of legends and stories as a small child, as well as authors such as Frank Edwards, John Keel, Charles Fort, Loren Coleman, Ivan Sanderson, Colin Wilson, and Nick Redfern.

His published books include Strange Things in the Woods (a collection of true, paranormal encounters) as well as the autobiographical My Strange World, where he talks about his own experiences dating back to childhood. Recently, he has written National Park Mysteries and Disappearances, Volumes 1, 2, and 3.

He also owns and narrates the wildly popular Among The Missing Youtube channel.

Also by Steve Stockton

13 PAST MIDNIGHT SERIES

MYSTERIES IN THE DARK SERIES

STRANGE THINGS IN THE WOODS

MY STRANGE WORLD

NATIONAL PARK MYSTERIES & DISAPPEARANCES
SERIES

Also by Free Reign Publishing

ENCOUNTERS IN THE WOODS

WHAT LURKS BEYOND

FEAR IN THE FOREST

INTO THE DARKNESS

ENCOUNTERS BIGFOOT

TALES OF TERROR

I SAW BIGFOOT

STALKED: TERRIFYING TRUE CRIME STORIES

MYSTERIES IN THE DARK

13 PAST MIDNIGHT

THINGS IN THE WOODS

CONSPIRACY THEORIES THAT WERE TRUE

LOVE ENCOUNTERS

STAT: CRAZY MEDICAL STORIES

CRASH: STORIES FROM THE EMERGENCY ROOM

LEGENDS AND STORIES: FROM THE APPALACHIAN TRAIL

BEYOND THE PATH: TRUE TALES OF TERROR IN THE WOODS: VOLUME 1

Printed in Great Britain
by Amazon